Whispers Of A Widowed Warrior

Dezarita Dashai

Based on a true story

Whisper Of A Widowed Warrior

By: Dezarita Dashai

Cover by Nay Cox

Logo Design: Angel Jones and Justin Ackerman

Editor: Anelda L. Attaway

© 2025 Dezarita Dashai

ISBN 978-1-965381-15-1

Library of Congress Control Number: ordered 2025919567

Whispers Of A Widowed Warrior

By: Dezarita Dashai

Epiphany:

For I am a modern-day Job, anointed and appointed to turn my tea into a testimony!

TURN THE PAGE AND ENJOY A SIP!

ACKNOWLEDGMENTS

I'd like to give all the glory to God! Thank You, God, for Your never-ending grace, for Your unlimited mercy, for the peace that surpasses all understanding. It is because of You that I can share my testimony!

To my boys:

How you all have made me proud! You've overcome so much in such a little time. There will be more battles for you to fight, more wars for you to win. While doing so, remember where your roots sprout (In God) and hold on tight to your faith. Remember to live for today, enjoying each moment. Yes, tomorrow isn't promised, but neither is today! I love you, I doooooo!

May the Lord cover you from the top of your head to the soles of your feet. Amen!

Philippines 4:13 NIV
I can do all things through Christ who strengthens me!
*In Jesus' Name! *

DEDICATION

I dedicate this book to grief in all its forms, as it presents itself.

The burdens you forced me to fit fell off! For I am a WARRIOR!

TABLE OF CONTENTS

INTRODUCTION

10 years ago!

"It's your wedding day; it's my wedding day.

It's our wedding day!

With this ring, I say I do.

I give my heart and my soul to you!"

-Three Piece-

I walked down the aisle, dressed in white. Swaying to the beat of India Arie, pouring my feelings out of my heart for all to hear, "Let me tell you why I love him. Because he is the truth. I said he is so real, and I love the way that he makes me feel. And if I am a reflection of him. Then I must be flying. Because his light shines so bright!"

There was my Superman, wrapped in white, chocolate melted just right from his nerves, waiting patiently. He slipped that beautiful ring onto my finger, and I lost it. There was a park full of people, yet none existed when we locked gazes.

Last night I dreamed, dreamed,

Yes, DREAMED of you.

Woke up thinking,

Did my dream REALLY come true?

Standing there holding my hand.

There was My DREAM MAN.

Kissing Me ALWAYS feels right.
I love how he WALKS AWAY when he's angry.
Not WANTING to fight.

Our love NEVER FELT SO GOOD!
Granting ALL my wishes…
Just like he said he WOULD.

Yes, Mr. Dream Man,
Clutching on so TIGHTLY to my hand.

Family Time is the KEY.
He's NEVER CONCERNED about himself,
IT'S ALWAYS WE.

Continuously meeting me halfway.
So I DON'T hesitate.
When he wants to Make Love
ON ANY GIVEN DAY.

He WALKS like a King in Grace.
Keeping that glowing smile ACROSS his face.
Bills CONSISTENTLY Paid On Time.
Treating Me like A QUEEN,
Giving me ALL of his spare time.

My DREAM MAN, Indeed.
I gave him the KEY to unlock me.
In his ARMS FOREVER
IS WHERE YOU CAN FIND ME!

Present Day!

Part One--194 days

Seasons Of Love:

525 thousand 600 minutes.

525 thousand moments so dear.

525 thousand 600 minutes

How do you measure a year?

How about love? Measure in love!

The Seasons of Love!"

-Jhonathan Larson-

SEPTEMBER 1, 2022:DAY 1

It's a full moon and a new moon all at the same time. The sky is extremely dark tonight, just like my energy. I'm tainted! The clouds that hover over our home are beginning to sink. The once white clouds reflecting the sun's beauty are now poisoned by dust and smoke! The dark gray shapes of despair are now holding drops of rain. Heavy, just like my soul feels. I am ready to release as an entire being! I gaze in awe at the illusion, which is a display of my world falling apart!

It is said that full moons signify clarity while heightening emotions and intuitions. New moons are to represent new beginnings, renewal, and growth. So, I ask, *"Where does that leave me?"* There I sat under such an illustration. Begging God for direction. Something has got my spirit in an uproar. I've always had a hard time getting out of bed, but this was different. I wasn't sure if I was coming or going these days. That wasn't me at all!

Yesterday, a thick, old White lady limped her way through my door. Flashing a Texas State license ID, she was wearing the title of my new childcare inspector. She demanded access to Ms. Dezy House of Love, my home childcare that I opened years ago. This was the home where Lavarious and I had fallen apart in a matter of days. There she stood with a look of disgust on her face. Plopping down to sit, the chair legs screamed for mercy into a bent-up position. Her red, flat face frowned as she requested my file folders.

"No biggie," I thought, *"All I need to do is remain calm. I am Ms. Dezy. I always keep my ducks in a row."* Then my heart dropped.

She slid her Glasses to the brim of her nose. "We received a complaint from your brother-in-law," she said, "You tried to kill him? Your husband fought him in the presence of children? Police were called to the scene. He's a resident yet not on any of your paperwork? No background check was done on this guy, so how do we know if he is cleared to be around children?" I tried to speak, but a cat had taken my tongue and tied that joker into knots!

"We have no Incident reports of police activity close to the children," she stated.

"Is it true that members of the mafia moved across from you, sold drugs, and participated in gang activity outside of the residence? You do realize how close all of this is to the presence of children, right?" I tried to calm my anxiety from taking over, but on and on she went.

"The police came to kick in their door. There was a back-and-forth open fire. Then your vehicle was stolen right out of your driveway?" she asked, "So, are these children really safe in your care? None of this was reported. Why is that, Miss Felton?"

I faded into the amygdala, the part of my brain where fear is soaked in. Yet there her lips kept moving. The frustration signals sent to my hypothalamus (which I allowed to oversee my nervous system) sent my blood pressure through the roof. Fight, flight, or freeze, they say. What about when you experience them all at once? Inflicting endeavoring wounds that would take decades to heal from.

I stood in front of her. Fighting myself with all the weapons I had, I insisted to myself not to smack her dead in her face. Finally, her lips sealed, waiting for my response. Her energy continued to attack me with allegations she had already accepted as truth before hearing a peep from me. There I froze, unable to articulate the nasty words I had for her unprofessionalism. Running in my head, away from myself, she clapped in my face.

"Mrs. Felton!" I looked at her with fury.

She smirked, wanting me to make a move. I contained myself.

"You are going to be cited for using the wrong form."

"The wrong form?" I echoed.

"I have been using this form since I opened my doors, and numerous inspectors have checked all my file folders yet said nothing about it."

"Yes, you will be getting cited for that, amongst several other things. This place is called. Ms. Dezy House of Love. It's your name that is on it, so it's all your responsibility to follow Texas State codes. No one else."

Tears rushed to my eyelids. I'm not sure if it was anger or sadness, or all the emotions crammed together. I just knew that I had to get away from around her. I kindly took my phone, put on some gospel music, and cleaned.

There, she stood and scribbled a book of tickets. Then shut me down!

"Lord, I told this man not to allow his brother back in here. First time, shame on him. Second time? Shame on us! Talking about, I tried to kill him? But did I, though?"

All I know is that into a superhero, I had to transform, yet again. Who else was gonna do it? I was left rescuing my boys from foolishness while my Superman was out being himself with the damn Car Clubs, in the community, and to everyone else. Hell. If I wasn't sure where to find him, I had to go look along the side of the highway! If a vehicle stalled out or anything. There was that damn Dub D's car decal on the back of his window. Superman to the rescue! He knew that it was okay because I wore a superwoman cape. I carried the world's burdens on my shoulders with a smile that never seemed to fade. So, I suppose I did it to myself.

The old runt called out, "Mrs. Felton!"

I suppose the gospel music got her together, or maybe she was just tired from tallying up my infractions. She really gave me an infraction for writing the names of my babies on their enrollment, instead of the form having it printed on there. This is unbelievable. But what could I do? Not a damn thing.

"Yes, Madam," I said.

I reported front and center with a smile I sometimes wished would take a damn break. She handed me a pen. I knew the routine. Signing my contract of suspension meant no daycare, no children, and no money! There, I signed my grants away; there, I signed my livelihood away. In depression, in a pile of bills, is the beginning of our end! I sank into a familiar hole. I grabbed liquor as a crutch to keep me as steady as I could be. I had no hope for our future. I relied on myself for so long. It seemed to be all I knew.

Now here I sat, below the moon and confused about what to do. I heard a faint whisper, "If he doesn't grow, it's time to go."

"Amen," I confirmed as I sat and recentered my world.

****

DAY 20

I walked in, to what seemed to be a dead house in my spirit. Why did it feel like no life resided here? Turning the corner, I witnessed the boys jumping on their dad as laughter filled the air. A familiar aroma hits my nostrils. On the stove, fried southern-style pork chops were one of my favorite meals. I sat and ate, grateful for the blessings that had been bestowed upon me in that very moment. Still, I wasn't satisfied. Instead, I felt drained and ashamed for feeling so depleted. The sad thing is, I didn't know why! I missed his warm embrace, wrapped with promises fulfilled. If only I could be as love-driven as he is. His heart was so big, so pure, so genuine. If only love were all that mattered the way it used to! Back then, love was my goal. I'd sit, gazing at the sky in gratitude. He'd ask time and time again:

"Bae, how do I make you feel?" Constantly looking at him and laughing, I gave no response.

He asked again, "Bae, how do I make you feel?"

"Hell, I don't know!"

Frustrated with my answer, he continued to do it my way. Waiting for me patiently, never going astray.

"Keeping it all on lockdown," thinking to myself, *"If I can control my*

own destiny, who can break my heart and turn my world upside down?"

You see, I have taken back MY KEY.
I sit back and enjoy the ride with a Great Big Smile.
Still, refusing to ALLOW my guards back down.

See, I Turned Over the Key
BACK OVER TO THE LORD.
Any man who wants it MUST GO THROUGH HIM,
NOT ME.

Captured by His Persistence, thinking to myself,
"What the heck is it?"

On and On he goes.
I thought, *"Is he putting on a show?"*
How in the World Do I Know?

Wanting to be seen for Me, and Only Me,
Was the Goal I STILL DIDN'T FOLD!

Here he went again,
"Bae, how do I make you feel?"
Trying to SHOO the Fluttering Butterflies Away.
But, then welcomed them to STAY.

Beginning to LATCH onto My Emotions.

It was TOO LATE.

My feelings reached an Unexplainable High,

Feens Go Missing to Reach.

Then it happened.

Baby, I Melted.

Melted like Marshmallows in Cocoa as he stirred me.

Stirred My Ying and My Yang,

YES, ALL OF ME!

Unshielded: My Heart.

My LOVE for him

All Over Again has TAKEN OVER my heart.

Determined to paint him a Wonderful Piece of Art.

I looked him in his Eyes.

Passion on the Rise

How do you make me feel, Bae?

You make me feel as if I am the Only Lady

Who WALKS this Earth.

When you Smile at Me with that flirty smirk.

Staring in My Eyes lets me know,

You feel as if you've WON the Ultimate Prize.

Showing me off WHEREVER we go.

Being sure to let the Whole World Know.

You make me feel just as Special as Our First Lady.

Got Me Feeling Like.

AYYYY!!! I RUN THIS BABY!

I'm shown your love in ALL You Do and Say.

Thank you for returning to Providing

From A-Z

You REALLY got me stunting on them.

"SINGING GET LIKE ME!"

Ha! Ha! Ha!

Wondering if God has SENT My Boaz AT LAST.

Holding and Kissing my Delectable Hand.

If I haven't told you already. I Love You So Much!

THANK YOU FOR BEING MY SUPERMAN!

But where was that man? Did my superwoman cape outshine his as we flew together? Did he retire, allowing me to take over purposefully? Did it become just too much of a hassle to take care of a damaged heart? I often wonder if I dragged him down with the baggage I took on from the world so gracefully. Did the bags that he added to my shoulders get too heavy for him to carry, as he held me in his arms? I'm not certain anymore, so I signed us up for therapy! Therapy focused on things irrelevant to me. I wanted to find out why Love was no longer enough for me! But they couldn't identify it either. Is it because we couldn't? All I could express was that I missed my Superman. All he could express was how, when he was standing right there! I suppose that alone was the problem.

A wonderful man stood before me. A man with no ill intentions against me. The best father ever. He earned the title of the "Boy's Knight in Shining Armor." They looked at him the way I longed to.

"I made you a drink, Bae."

"I'll drink it later," I said, fighting tears of confusion.

Back to the place that knew me best: my bed. Bed rotting was one of my favorite activities. Praying and praying that the sounds of joy from the boys and their dad would contaminate my soul, wishing it would bite me so I could transform into exactly who they needed me to be. But I couldn't, I didn't know how. Instead, I cried and wrote, then cried some more.

Hours later, I noticed these 280 pounds 5-11 forming a shadow before me.

"HR messed up my money again."

Showing me proof on his phone, the disappointment in his eyes mirrored mine. Jumping up, anxiety fueled my feet to the door.

"It's not my fault, Bae; they keep messing up."

I stood in the doorway, showing my humanity, showing my weakness. Tear knots caught in my throat. Water waves raced down my face.

No longer did I want to be held, rocked back and forth. No longer was I interested in him praying over me as church hymns were sung. The comfort that lay in his arms was no longer enough. I wanted a check that I could take to the bank and then wait for my change. Just as he promised me. Another promise made reality, so all is fine. But his glance showed how defeated he was.

"I know, Lavarius, it never is!" Closing the door behind me, he caught the latch.

"Where are you going, Dez?" A look of fury flashed across his face.

"To get some air," I responded.

It may not have been time to go, but I didn't stick around to entertain it! In my car, I jumped. Speeding on down the road, in search of some sort of release. I wanted as many shots as my body would allow! I knew just where to go to vent, be loved on, and have a great time. My boo Bianca! He grew to despise her. She always came to rescue me. I was secretly a train wreck, but I continuously showed up for the world. I needed to be poured back into. Somehow. Someway. I set out to fill an unidentified void. Being away from my own home became the shield that I needed to hide from my own issues. When the energy became too heavy, when thoughts consumed me, and when answers I needed to be answered, couldn't be answered by anyone, (not even myself!) I ran and hid away.

Leaving the boys with Lavarius wasn't an issue, which made it easier for me to run! He loved those jokers. Took them to Car Club shows. Play nerfs gun wars with them. I'd give him the best dad of the year repeatedly. It was me, all me. In this funk I stayed, losing myself. Yet, this world had no idea. There I was, still smiling! Lending this splintered soul of mine to put smiles on others' faces, making the world a better place. I became less available to him. I faked it till I made it, so of course, no one noticed. I started meeting my own needs, no longer requiring anything nor accepting anything from him! I had no words to utter, yet my silence was so loud. I checked out completely. Taking my barrier home and hiding behind it. I disappeared inside of myself. I missed who I used to be but had no idea how to return there. Before I knew it. I got addicted to just existing. So much so, I decided there was no growth, and it was time to go.

Time flew by. It was day 45! With an empty void in one hand and a bottle of Tequila in the other. I moved half of the boys and me into a one-bedroom house. We moved into a one-bedroom house. A permanent break that I would finally be able to receive. Well, so I thought!

****

DAY 63

I stared out at the cloud-filled sky through the window. The sun was setting behind the clouds, the birds flying, and singing to the flaps of their own wings. If only I could trade spots with them! Freedom was what I yearned for. I was still unsure about how to obtain it, though. Instead, I was thinking about how I just dropped his boys off at his dad's house. He lived there and, of course, didn't want them dropped off. That was a first, only because we seemed to have it in for each other. We bickered back and forth. Petty Betty versus Petty Bobby. Salty at the fact that we both wore smiles without the other. Feelings were hurt from past actions that bled out. Saying things we didn't mean out of the frustration of being apart. It all got so old so fast. Things separated, once bought together. Empty threats delivered. The separation of a union once joined as one.

"It's okay," I'd utter to myself as I hide behind my shield unbothered.

My only goal was to do what I always do: make stuff happen for these boys. Which I did! <u>ALL</u> of them! The Lord blesses me with the grant approval. Finally, off suspension. Finally, able to keep children again under different regulations. That means less children, less money. But I was grateful. I went home to celebrate.

For the first time, my family saw me in a different light. For 10 years, I wore the reflection of my husband, of my boys, and of the burdens I carried upon my shoulders for this entire world! They were expecting my smile to be dimmed with all that I had encountered. What they didn't see was that it was on the inside. Hollow, yet full of heartbreak, to keep it from showing on my face, I kept drinking. I just wanted to party and forget about it all for a moment. I wanted the smile I wore to be a true representation for a change. So, I smiled, I smiled, and I smiled again.

Love does not dissipate in 63 days! Not even with the foolishness. We kept up the mess. His stepmother and father, at one point, felt I was the reason for this whole thing. I can't say I didn't feel that way sometimes. So, I left it at that.

My Suga Serenna kept my hair done, and she was sure to keep my spirits high. Random songs, messages, and nights out to hear me vent reminded me that I could feel exactly how I needed to feel, and I did. I loved and missed him dearly. I went back and forth behind my shield about my decision! Stuck with no answer, just longing to go back to what was familiar. In comparison to this new door, I've plowed into. It had been a roller coaster so far. Inflation had eaten up my bank account. The very hole

I worked so hard to get out of. I was living paycheck to paycheck, unable to do as I pleased when I wanted to. One thing about me, I'm willing to work my tail off to get it all back, was an understatement. Yet, I was still unsure of anything. All God said was to keep smiling in gratitude, even when I felt I couldn't! So that is just what I did.

I could only party for so long with my family. Reality was beating at my door, and so were the calls from Lavarius that I ignored. He probably thought that I was 1000 miles away in a guy's bed. I definitely was seeing what I could see. But I never did what I could do. I focused on making memories with my family. I got hugs from everyone before my departure day came.

"Until next time, family," I pushed out. Back to reality, I flew.

****

DAY 83

The bathroom walls yelled at me.

"Your husband would never allow you to get this drunk! He would have made you a drink but fed you good, so you weren't sick like this. Drugs? That's what you call being free? You shouldn't have left him to begin with!"

"Where am I?" I spoke back to the walls.

Closing my eyes tightly. Looking for an answer behind them.

"Fuck!" I exclaimed, spinning in chaos.

A knock on the door followed by a man's voice answered me.

"Open the door, Dez."

"Lavarius?" I was ashamed, unable to talk from the cotton stuffed in my mouth. I stumbled to the door stall and unlocked it.

"Thank you, Chastity, for callin'!" He shouts out to my home girl sitting on the bench in the bathroom.

"What the hell took place?" That is the look I gave her.

She and I met when I started working third shift at the Amazon airport. I suppose we call ourselves being grown. At least I did. Taking a THC gummy while drinking on an empty belly almost took me out of this world. Scooping me up in his arms, my body went slumped. I fell asleep on his shoulder, woke up to his hands touching my body. His lips met mine. An explosive vault of ecstasy came over me. Satisfied, he left my body. Regret stained my heart. The love he somehow transferred into me, gone by mourning with a blazing headache to accompany it. There, Bianca came to my rescue, nursing me back to health. Spilling all the beans had me singing. Maybe it's true, love doesn't live here anymore.

****

DAY 120

T he brisk air blew the sediments of our dimmed fire to blaze. It ignited my tears along with it. I hid under a black hoodie that seemed 2 sizes too big, yet that belonged to me for years. Tucked in the hammock, I swung to the beat of emotions that I couldn't make out. What is this feeling? The man who made me his wife 10 years ago, the same man whose descriptions of me amounted to a sorry wife, yet who loved me so much, was standing over me, uttering words. I used to think about those 10 years and get angry. I poured out vulnerability, laying my flawed being front and center. How self-absorbed of him to require abundance from me.

Yet the moment I began to meet such desires, he reciprocated with cynical energy! It had me questioning. Did he even want me?

That one question amplified so loudly in my mind. Its bass swallowed each syllable he spoke. Sitting up to ground myself. I let the earth pull me out of my head through my feet.

"Dez, Dez." Finally hearing his stern voice of stillness.

I noticed the glass. His huge hands were covered. I grabbed it with gratitude. Latching on to the other hand. We exchanged glances as the heat projecting off his hands met my ice-cold fingers. Was he trying to make out a description of this very moment as well?

120 days of despair, desperation, yet determination. It almost made me forget how much he truly cared for me. It was I who became subject to weariness, the task of carrying the load for so many years. It broke me down real bad. Flight. Flight or freeze, they say. I took flight with the prayer that he'd come fight for me. Here it was 120 days later. I sat there frozen. Superwoman cape in one hand, a painted-on smile in the other, ready to be properly planted in its position.

"Dez! Dez!"

"Yes, Sir," I responded.

"Put your shoes on, nut!" he yelled.

The glimpse of his smile gave me one as the lyrics from my speaker sang out.

"I will do anything for you. You are my life. That's one thing that's true."

It's been 37 days since I've seen the joy he wears. I wondered if he knew this song was how a part of me feels. How there wasn't a fire too hot for me to run across for him, for me, for us. I was just at a point where I needed him to run through the fire. For me, for him, for us. Before that, part of me was no more. That part of me was still hanging on by a thread, longing for him to come rescue me, as he once did as my Superman. However, I can only hold on for so long.

Unable to differentiate anything. Stuck in silence, scared to speak. I said my good nights. My impulses only brought me abrupt satisfaction. What I required lasted a lifetime.

****

DAY 121

I know this joker got a little girlfriend. Heck, so do I. But why am I his first thought? And he is mine when we rise with the sunrise. Like teacups on the boy's favorite ride, around we went. It didn't work. Waiting for the other to make the next move. Whatever that was. I stood waiting for time. I longed for him to realize he needed me, while longing for me to get past it all and let him move on so he could just be.

On a break to see if what was broken could be mended. He was sitting with words I threw at him from the residue of his actions swept under the rug. Then the moment I claimed not to care, I tripped over all of my trauma. That fall landed me in the courthouse asking for divorce papers. Open wounds bleed each time I ask him to sign. I figured he had a little girlfriend, so he'd be fine.

Fighting my own voice, telling me to go back and make the first move. He will get it together. We will no longer be in lack!" I responded to myself.

That's JUST TOO MANY REASONS for Me.

I ONLY NEED ONE!

WHICH WAS ME!

Again, I spoke. Just be Patient.

He will get it Together.

What about the boys?

He Loves You, you know that.

You have a Beautiful Family.

God is going to Turn that Thing Around.

Just Go Back, Stay. Make it Work!

I said: That's JUST TOO MANY REASONS for Me.

I ONLY NEEDED ONE.

WHICH WAS ME.

You see,

As long as My Cup was full

I poured out to Everything and Everybody.

Then I RAN OUT OF LOVE.

Switch Turned Off, Drained, Depleted, Burned Out.

I WAS ON E.

I NEEDED you for me,

To Come and Save My Day

SOMEHOW, SOME WAY.

But there I was, Still Holding

My Superwoman Cape.

By then, I knew it was TOO LATE.

Because I began Running On Fumes.

For sure, I knew,

Honey, we were in a Lose-Lose.

Maybe I am HINDERING you.

Maybe you are HINDERING Me!

Maybe the Clock has Expired.

OUR LUCK RAN OUT!

Maybe you'll COME BACK to Me.

And I'll COME BACK to You.

We will be HEALED with overflowing cups

READY TO REBUILD.

You know what I said?

That's just TOO MANY REASONS for Me.

I ONLY NEEDED ONE.

WHICH WAS ME!

Sometimes,

We try to take

Everything and Everyone with us.

Then Our Life becomes a fuss.

We tend to Love Them

For them, Till Death

But in the End…

We are the Ones

That Runs Out of Breath.

Telling ourselves.

I WILL Be Blessed for this.

God will send me JUST ONE MORE WISH.

Love WINS at the End of the Day.

But you know what I say:

That is JUST TOO MANY REASONS for Me.

AND I ONLY NEEDED ONE.

And that Reason…

WAS ME!

****

DAY 122

Here come those loud ass pipes. I sat on my wrapped porch full of impatient flowers, watching the chocolate melt off him as he jammed out to those Southern soul Blues. I couldn't take my eyes off him even after he brought his truck to a halt. I watched him open his door through the window. It gave me a smile knowing the question I was going to ask, as well as the answer I was going to receive.

He did that bowleg walk on over to me, and I smirked out, "With all that money you got, you need to get that raggedy truck fixed."

Laughing my tail off. Our synchronized answers slipped out together.

"I told you it's under construction."

"Yeah, Yeah, Yeah!" I called back.

"Dawg, I sure am hungry!" I whined out.

Validation glowed on his face as he handed me a plate.

"Let me know when you're ready for dessert," he winked.

"Boy gone on," sped from my tongue.

We let out chuckles in the air as he watched me devour fried pork chops. So hot that I could still taste the grease. Just how I like it. If he did nothing else, this man made sure we ate. During this separation, my soul wasn't the only thing crying out for him like a puppy panting for water after a walk. In the mirror, I watched as my body weight declined. I yearned to be loved like this again. Hearing my body crying out for the nutrients it relied on from my Superman did something to me. Not sure why I was wired this way. When I experienced any discomfort in life, stress, anxiety, or blood pressure elevation, my appetite disappeared. I became vulnerable to his ways, ready to throw myself at him, but I couldn't. No way was I gonna admit any of that, so I popped my tongue halfway through.

"It wasn't all of that. I have had better. You slipping, Homie!"

Laughing with fragments of deliciousness, digesting, saturating my entire GI tract. It gave me comfort right then and there, yet still I said nothing.

How baffling is it to have desires and not express them? To have a listening ear but refuse to allow your request to fall upon them. It's in me, not on me. It's all I could say in defense. My belief system was so strong. No way could I give the manual to my heart to be followed. I wanted him to meet my needs. Because he wanted to, just as he used to. Fly in and save the day, make this separation not be in vain. I didn't want him to leave; I wanted him to stay.

"Alright, Dez. We have a Car Club meeting, I'll hit you later."

His fabricated embrace told on him. He didn't hear my inner voice contemplating its next steps. I took what I could get and kept it moving.

"Alright then, thank you so much for the food," I said.

"Yup!" he called out from behind him as he jumped back to that raggedy old truck.

****

DAY 157

This man's not cutting my grass, right? Lavarious would never. Now he has missed an entire patch over there.

"Ohh no! My goodness," I peered out the window, fussing, "Let me go call Lavarius, he is scheduled to wash my car this week anyway. I know he's waiting on the money."

My feet hurried across the floor, anxious to hear him grant my request, but before I could demand Siri to call my husband.

It yelled back at me, "Call from SIS!"

I answered the phone to a bunch of static wrapped in broken syllables and distress. It was sent to my heart on a race against my mind.

"Grandma was rushed to the hospital and now she's on life support."

My words stuck in traffic, unable to make it to my lips. To the bathroom, I ran away from the boys. I sobbed quietly. No way is this true. We texted daily. The last few days, she hadn't responded. How didn't I know something was wrong? My granny was young, beautiful, mobile, and independent. You mean to tell me a fall in the tub burst an aneurysm in her brain, no one knew anything about? Suddenly, just like that, she was gone out of my life. She raised me, instilled morals and values that I hold dearly. She rooted for Lavarius but stood by my side, never judged me, even while knowing the entire truth! Just like that, she was brain-dead over 1000 miles away. I was distraught, sinking fast in a hole I dug for myself 157 days ago.

I said a prayer with my Sis, and we ended the call. In my bed, I rotted cautious of my energy because I still was a mother. I needed to be held, comforted, loved on, and understood. Calling my friend would be detrimental to my health. She already deemed me weak in her book for feeling so many emotions that I couldn't identify. I knew who to call. My Superman. The bear tone in his voice when he answered sent me into a panic. Unable to get a word out between the breaths, I tried to catch. The shortness of air fueled knots in my throat, forcing tears to stream down my face. Unable to speak, I hung up and ran out of the house to ensure my boys weren't contaminated by my energy.

Ten minutes later, I heard those pipes miles away headed in my direction. He pulled up alongside me. I stopped walking just in time for his bear arms to hug me to my knees. I allowed all the hurt from this entire thing to plunge into him. From the fussing to the boys being separated, to us being a permanent stain in my memory. I missed him, I missed us, I missed my Granny! My body went limp. Scooping my small frame up onto his shoulders, he carried me to the truck. His speakers normally vibrated my body as I fussed, but this time, he left it completely silent.

Arriving at my house, he made sure to light a fire before placing me in my hammock. There, I let out yelps of exhaustion. An emotional release, because this was all too much for me. He stared at me. Despair from me now transferred to him. Regrets took over me.

"I will take off work and drive you. I got you," kissing my forehead.

Walking over to reposition the logs on the fire. I watched him. Just as the fire grew, anger grew in me. I paid $1200 for a one-bedroom where those boys slept on the couch; I worked at the daycare during the day and at Amazon overnight to take care of us. My income reduced significantly due to not being able to have the full capacity of children. I knew his situation. Staying with his dad, trying to make ends meet just as I am. The statement he just made echoed back to me.

"I will take off work and drive you to Green Bay, WI."

I knew he meant every word. He loved me wholeheartedly. But how in the hell were we going to get there? With the funds I came up with, of course. The anger in me took over, and an uncontrollable scream escaped the dark pits I hid them in. All I wanted was for the man I married, my Superman, my husband. Who now stood over me in confusion. To show up when I couldn't, for me, for us, for the boys, for this family. He reached his arms out to touch my body, but in a fetal position, I froze.

Unable to articulate anything but: "We can't be anymore; you aren't what I need you to be. I apologize. I allowed our connection to shrink, then, in return, I couldn't be what you needed. Isn't that why you labeled me a sorry wife?"

"What are you talking about, Dez?" he spoke.

I set up wiping the pain from my eyes.

"I am talking about how you need to sign these papers. We need to end this," I demanded.

"But I love you."

"I love you too, Lavarius." The sting of pain burned my cheekbones as they fell so rapidly.

Still, I continued to plead my case. "Please. Let's just knock it all down and build a new foundation. If it's meant for us to be, we will be. What we need to do is focus on bettering ourselves. We can always get remarried. It's just a piece of paper."

"You know I am not trying to do that. I love you. I thought we were just taking a break," he defended.

"Yes, that does not have to change. Maybe we need to take a real break. Let go of what was, so we can focus on what will be. We always can get remarried, Lavarius. What else is there to do?"

"Dez, I really am not trying to do that!" He became definite in his body language.

"Is this really all his ass had to say?" I lost my composure even more and yelled:

"Why do you want me? Didn't you say I was a sorry wife? What, because I allowed stress to isolate me into a corner where intimacy never lay for you? No, I wasn't perfect, I've grown expediential in the last 10 years! But I was the sorry wife? Bro, I took all your betrayals with a grain of salt. Grinning and bearing the weight of it all! The Car Club World, funky town, the boys and all your fuckin' side pieces got my Superman! You put your cape on and up and away you went. Well fuck that! I was your wife! Not them! So excuse the hell out of me for finally running out of fuel after all this damn time! I am exhausted, Lavarius! I'm tired. We have got to let go!" With tears in his eyes, pride hurt deep beneath the shadows of his soul.

Pain shifted off his tongue, "Please, just hold on, I'm going to show you." In an attempt to block our pain from becoming one, I stopped him abruptly.

"Show me than Lavarius!" Taking the paper out of my car, with a pen, he signed on the dotted line.

"I love you so much, Lavarius!" I smiled as tears fell into the laugh lines he once adored.

"No, you don't, I am trying my best. Like what you want from me?"

What I wanted to say was: "I wanted to be as vulnerable as I was when you became my husband. I used to cry in your arms as you rocked me. I was safe, protected, I was your wife! When you told me you were going to do something."

It DIDN'T RETURN to me voided.

You were My Superman.

Then Broke My Heart Repeatedly.

I FORGAVE YOU!

But,

It created a Void

That I'm Unable to Fill.

What I wanted to say was:

I WANTED You to Fight longer than

A Few Months Consistently.

I WANTED you to Show Up

And Make Us One Again

To figure it out WITHOUT ME

And LEAD as you used to,

I NEVER WANTED this to go this far.

I NEVER WANTED to Lose You-Us-

This Family We Built Together!

I JUST WANTED you to grow.

NO TALK! ALL SHOW!"

But, instead,

The other voice in my head told me:

Maybe what I wanted is Selfish!

Maybe

We JUST AREN'T MEANT for Each Other.

Maybe

I Missed Out on a Great Guy

I don't know!

But hey,

THIS IS WHAT I WANTED, RIGHT?

I looked at him with a face that had so much yet nothing to say. Trying to keep his composure, away he went, who knew that would be the last time?

****

DAY 172

He no longer sent me heartfelt messages in the morning; I no longer expected them. I was living in a toxic moment with my friend, and he was in a co-dependent one with his! Reflecting on his words: *"What you want from me?"* Why didn't I answer? I could have given him a rundown of such. Because the voices in my head still fought me to make the first move. Maybe it was no longer about what I wanted from him at that moment! It was too many reasons for me, and I only needed one. Me!

My phone chirped: **Lavarius:** "I talked to your Auntie; she wants the boys again for spring break. If you drive them, I'll pay for the gas."

Me: "Okay, deal!"

Lavarius: "How much you want?"

Me: "250 bucks."

Lavarius: "Really? That's what we doing now?"

Me: "You asked, so I answered."

The bubbles bubbled on his end. I waited in anticipation, ready to fuss. Laughing to myself. Then there was nothing. I guess he didn't feel like fussing with me today.

"I'll catch him later," I whispered to myself jokingly.

Well, I did. 6:30 pm rolled around, and there he came calling. I answered.

Me: "Yes, Sir?"

Him: "What you doing, Otis?" I could hear his smile from ear to ear.

Me: "Nothing, cleaning up this Lil Boy mess."

Him: "Oh, okay, how you holding up? How's your grandma doing?"

Me: "It's my grandma's birthday today, but they still haven't taken her off that machine. Holding on with every ounce of hope left in them, I suppose. I just feel she's suffering."

Him: "Won't you let me drive you there so you can say goodbye?"

Me: "I've already made my peace with her soul transitioning. That is just a shell that no longer mirrors her beautiful appearance; she kept up so well."

Now she lay there all swollen with machines and wires crisscrossed over her. Absolutely no brain activity at all. I wish they'd just let her rest! But who am I to advise anything when I am all the way here? I don't want to go see that. I'm never going back to that place.

Feeling suddenly heavy, we're pose to be playing on the phone as we had made a habit of fussing just because, it put a smile on both our faces. We were starting all the way over with no baggage. But there I was, unpacking on him! Unable to control my emotions. I hung up on him.

"Text message from Lavarius," Siri yelled, "Dang, it's like that!"

Me: "I'm so sorry, I didn't mean to do that. I need to be by myself. My apologies, take care."

Him: "No response."

He wasn't a stranger to my isolation. Ten years gave him lots of practice. He knew when my energy was off, I stayed in the cut. Except this time, it was different. Back to the hole I went, sinking further. My friend. She was just a distraction. Something I thought was real turned out to be a counterfeit, keeping me afloat. Though giving me some sort of relief, I needed to remember the hole was not where I belonged. I accepted a pretend life with her that I didn't want. I accepted it because what else was there? Lavarius started to focus more on his friend. Checking in every now and then to see if I had changed my mind. I wanted to tell him as soon as he moved out of his dad's house, got himself together, I'd be right there in his arms. But I waited. Telling myself as I always have. If it's meant to be, it will be!

****

DAY 187

The sun woke me as I stretched out on the couch with my friend. House was all we played, and I have to say I fell victim to its concept. I forgot how to be me, didn't care to find her either. Bruised, broken, and beaten down. Searching for this void to be filled somehow, someway. Sometimes I thought she was the love of my life; other times, I told myself to enjoy the ride, because every other day her actions showed otherwise. But there I sat under her as if this was just the beginning.

My phone buzzed, "I got two big moving jobs that're like $2000 each, and that apartment has openings. You still gonna help me with the application?"

I responded so quickly, "I got you."

From that point, I was on cloud 9 all day. Lavarius was really about to come and get me! Finally, our family would be one again. My heart flashed back to how he took our boys to car shows, buying them all the snacks he saw. I was spoiled. I sat at the house, sunbathing in peace, grounding my entire naked body on the soft grass he planted with his rigid hands. Flashes of the night we played Pity-Pat, our go-to card game. We sang karaoke and danced the night away. I heard my heartbeat for a man who loved me and I him.

Snap, Snap, Snap, my mind snapping its fingers at me to exit La La Land, to remember my reality. Love is great, yes, but love isn't enough. We've already established this fact.

"Get it together! It demanded!" My smile faded, and my anxious thoughts took over.

I searched for liquor to calm me. Confused, angry, yet hopeful of a future to come. All I had to do was wait. Maybe he'd finally come through.

Or maybe I'll be stuck in this circle of lust, maybe love, and fun, then toxicity takes over all categories! I suppose I'd become a pro at playing house. Waiting on it to end, so I could return safe and sound to my Superman. Well, that's if he was coming to get me!

****

DAY 194

As she walked out my door. I looked at the dim light on my phone signaling its battery life.

"4:00 am. Sheesh," I spoke surprisingly.

It seemed I just closed my eyes. *"Who in the world is this man?"* I asked myself.

I was sleeping so well that I didn't hear my phone chirp at me. So many missed calls from Facebook Messenger. Curious about which scammer decided to try to bother me overseas. I opened it up to see. Never expecting to see the words that almost stopped my heart: Lavarius Davis was in a bad wreck on Highway 20. In Arlington by the Highlands. I was trying to tell his family.

"An accident?" I whispered in confusion.

I called him back. "Hi, you called me and..." before I could get another word out, he interrupted.

"I was trying to get a hold of Lavarius Davis' family."

"Yes, I am his wife. What's going on?"

"He was in a bad wreck on Route 20 in Arlington by the Highlands. I see it all over my feed and wanted to reach out."

"Thank you!" was all I could spit out as I jumped out of my bed, panicking.

I know he still lived with his dad, so that was my first point of contact.

"Mr. Vaugh, Lavarius there?"

"I'm at the Game Room, Sweetie. Call Carla."

Following directions, I did just that. Receiving no for an answer! Right then, I spilled the beans and told her the news I had received. Still in disbelief. I had to investigate to be certain.

"Was this him? Could it have been a pure mix-up? Could it have been a misunderstanding? It could not have possibly been him. Or was it?"

To Facebook, I ran to get a hold of a few of his side pieces. The founder of his Car Club, Dub D's, called me back.

I gave him the information: "Apparently, he was coming home from work, then something so sudden happened. I don't know if it's his truck, but I'm about to call all the hospitals."

His voice held worry, fear, and anxiety about what was to come. Adding onto mine, I accepted his energy, yet I was still in denial. Calling hospitals near Highway 20 to scan for his arrival.

"No! We have no one here by that name."

On to the next, I called. "No, Ma'am, he isn't in our care."

Then, finally, "Repeat that name for me…" she paused with conviction as I heard her eyes scan the information so loudly.

My heart skipped a beat. I heard it loud and clear. "Yes, Ma'am, we do have him in our care, and you are?"

"His wife!" The title slipped off my tongue with ease: "Get here as soon as you can."

She spat out, "He is in critical condition."

Still unable to accept such news, while being frightened all at the same time. His dad and I followed up with the Car Club about his whereabouts. No answer. The sun started to peek its head from the clouds. I stood on my porch for a hot second, silently begging its presence to heal me.

Then the phone rang: "Sweetie!" he paused. The panic I felt echoed in my eardrums as he continued to speak.

"It is him! I went over to the scene to check. I saw his truck upside down with his car club decal on the back window. I spoke to the officers on the scene; they told me they took him to Arlington Memorial Hospital."

We spoke out in unison. "Yes, I spoke to a lady at the hospital. She says he's in critical condition and we need to get there quickly."

I spoke, "Critical condition?" His words bounced off the fear that had taken over him. In unison, we became once again.

"I'm on the way."

"Critical condition. Ohh God no, no God, please don't let it be."

His dad beat me to the hospital, then in came his stepmom. Next came his aunt. Soon, we had a waiting room full of family and friends sitting in anxiety, trying not to allow it to consume us. Pappi, my oldest son, has been calling nonstop. He woke up to my empty bed. What else could I do?

"I am out Ubering for those shoes you want. Be home soon!" Send! Oh, how I wish that were true.

I'd take the disgusting smells of random foods I picked up just to drop off 10 minutes away over this feeling. The truth was, I sat there in limbo, trying to control my thoughts so they didn't overwhelm me. Out walks the doctor with two surgeons and the chaplain. Before he could get anything out. His aunt lost her composure.

"Ohh no, he's gone, he's gone, he's gone!" Her words of agony pierced my numbness, yet I sat oblivious to her.

As well as my own reactions. I had to know what he had to say. I zoned in, I listened carefully, following every syllable that came out of his mouth.

"He suffered blunt trauma to vital organs. When we wheeled him in, he was conscious, and his vitals weren't too bad. However, the moment we got him upstairs, he went right into cardiac arrest…"

Pausing for a reaction from me or anyone else, I gave him nothing but silence. Others nodded in understanding. I sat on the edge of my seat listening for more, waiting patiently for the part where he spoke.

"He's all better now. Feel free to take him home. The Chaplain only came out to pray with you all, to encourage you all to be grateful for such a miracle."

"Nope! I wasn't that lucky." The deep sigh he gave caused me to fight the elevator, raising my blood pressure levels.

"We were able to go in and stop the bulk of the bleeding," he said.

I looked deep in his eyes to latch on to any ounce of hope. I needed it. I had to keep it together because once I lost it, that was it.

"He's a strong, healthy big fella. I believe he's gonna pull through."

I took his words as ammunition, shooting tears away. I prayed, prayed, and prayed. The long seconds turned into excruciating hours. I collected fragments of hope flying around as his car club walked in. Giving fake hugs and no updates, with only my physical being intact, raised a few eyebrows. Completely numb! Emotionless!

More hours passed. I walked over to get coffee when one of Big Country's partners approached me. His warm embrace carried whispers.

"After Big Country pulls through this, y'all need to stop this mess and work it out."

That was the last straw that broke this camel's back. I chanted, walking back to my seat.

"He's going to be okay. He's going to be okay. God, please let him be okay." Time didn't move as fast as my emotions.

Although I tried dragging them right along with it. I failed at such a mission. A few minutes later, I broke. Into the bathroom I bolted. Yelps are finally free from the bondage I held them in. I shook uncontrollably. In rushed Ms. Carla, in rushed the secretary from the Car Club, along with whomever else. Last thing I knew: my legs came unfastened from this earth. I lost control of my breathing. So many thoughts I kept hidden flooded my mind. A winner escaped my lips.

Placed on repeat: "He has to be okay. We were so close. Please God. Please!" The rest is a blur.

Unaware of how I came out of it. Back in the waiting room, I sat. I heard shallow, fuzzy words in the distance. Lots of them. Yet, only one sentence in particular was able to beat down the door I hid behind. Forcing my head to follow its path. I told him to stay the night. We were all drinking. I'm just glad Jaylon wasn't in the car. He stayed.

The words came out of his play sister's mouth. Confused, frustrated, and embarrassed, I didn't utter a word. I explained what I felt happened because this is my husband, right? There was no secret about our separation, which meant, in reality, I had no clue of his whereabouts, of the situation, of anything. Yet, I took responsibility. How foolish of me to explain what happened to my knowledge! What's even more foolish is that everyone knew what happened but me. They continued to let me think he was coming home from work. I knew his schedule. He worked late; he'd blast his music to keep himself awake. That raggedy truck was all metal. A Chevy Yukon, that was "under construction!" He drove with speed yet smarts! He was behind a car that must have done a brake check while he looked down at his phone to change his music or to text me, or his friend, or his mother. Looking up in time to swerve left to prevent all that metal from hitting the car in front of him. Because of his speed, he went over the cement barricade, splitting off the opposite lane, where he landed for God knows how long in pain and suffering. Later, another truck going at a fast speed hit him again, knocking him back into the cement barricade. That is what the detective told me. I mean, of course, I inserted my own pieces to fill in the blanks, but why couldn't that story be true? Before I knew it, I spoke with firm anger in my voice.

"So you mean to tell me y'all was getting drunk and let y'all let him leave?"

"Now you know Country get everyone else drunk, but be sipping himself." My anger grew.

Needing something tangible to blame, I frowned. "Still!" I blurted out!

"Davis!" the doctor called out! I jumped up, "You can see him now." We all started walking.

"Only 4-5 at a time," he called back! Me, his dad, stepmom, auntie, brother, and uncle went.

How I ached for Ms. Leeann and Britney. His mom and sister, who would kill a brick for him. They were six hours away in Arkansas, making their way here as soon as they found out. The separation put some distance between us, but the boys were always their priority. All four of them. I tried to imagine their pain at that very moment. I couldn't imagine them hearing dreadful syllables from Mr. Vaughan. It had to have ripped at their eardrums. That was her baby boy, her heart. Nothing stopped her from coming to Texas for her fat baby. Now here we were. To the elevator we walked, silence screamed the pants off our breath, blending into fear. What were we walking into? The doctor said nothing, just continued to lead us down the hall! Beeps, chords, nurses, doctors, all around a 5 by 8 room. He lay there. Or was it him? Swelling changed the chocolate in his face that I once admired. Tubes clouded the succulent lips I avoided.

"Lavarius, you know I don't kiss. Shoot, I don't know where them lips been."

"Girl gone," he'd reply as I forced my jaw to a bite, followed by a smirk, "Ohh, you know where they've been."

If we did nothing else, we fussed and had fun. Those combinations may have been the very sound keeping us connected as one. Now all I heard were beeps combined with rapid heart rates from all of us. No words were spoken, just intense thoughts colliding with each other. In rushed the nurses, doctors, and the whole team.

"His organs ruptured from the blunt force he experienced. But we're working hard to get him stable," he updated.

Why didn't we wear seatbelts? That was a practice we never put into play. The ding of the seat belt notification became a tune we sang along to each time we rode. Heck, most of the time that fat baby rolled right in the front alongside him. Inseparable, I tell you. From the day I gave birth, Ahkhim knew his daddy to be his everything.

On his belly, he lay. On his belly, he walked. On his belly, he illustrated a creative obstacle course for his cars to go through. The funny thing is, Lavarius Fat Tail lay there sleeping, allowing him to do as he pleased. Because that was his fat baby indeed. Blood was forced into his IV. They poured and poured and poured. Levels dropped, then rose. I couldn't take it anymore. I needed to see his eyes meet mine one last time.

In his ear, I whispered, "Wake up. Stop playing Ottis." Then walked back to my X, as another loved one exited theirs.

We took turns whispering sweet nothings in his ear, praying for a sign of relief. Then came the doctor to elaborate on his entire situation. The hope I once hung on to dissipated into the tears I shed listening to his words.

"We lost him twice, but there's an amazing team giving it their all. We just haven't been able to stop the bleeding completely."

"I'm sorry," he dragged from his lips as he offered condolences, walking away within a matter of seconds.

His monitor sprang out in chaos. There, we watched his heartbeat rapidly as it dropped. On top of him, the nurse jumped, plunging into him.

"He's back! Yes!" she yelled!

Then again, she yelled in panic! On and on they administered CPR, switching positions, pumping him so hard I'm sure his ribs were broken. I had no more whispers to hand out.

I screamed, "Fight Lavarius, Fight! Your fat baby needs you. Please! What am I going to tell the boys?"

Back again he came, and then again went the machines. In an uproar, my body, adrenaline pumping, my next thoughts into the future.

"Is this my truth? Am I about to lose him for good?" I can't bear to see

him take his last breath.

Out of here I must go. A kiss I laid upon his forehead as they stood on standby for his soul to transition. It wasn't supposed to end like this.

"Goodbye, Superman. I love you." Out I walked.

Walking as fast as my limber legs could carry me, I hit the escape button only to be caught by another one of his Car Club members.

"Country gone?" they asked.

Before I could give an answer, my body wins against the force of gravity. My legs no longer could support such a mass of stress. Out like a light I went. Coming to, in a chair, I sat.

"What happened?" I asked.

Her sweet energy comforted me, and she prayed over me.

"We knew what y'all were going through. But I want to tell you something. I talked to Country on several occasions. One thing he made clear is how much he loved his wife! That man loved you, Sis." I heard another member say.

The Car Club I once despised came through for me. I listened to all their words of wisdom pour into me. The alarms of anxiety blared. In pecked his mother. Overtaken by tears, held up by Britney. A crunch barley stable herself. Unaware that his soul had already transitioned. She raced to her son's side in slow motion, collapsing on his lifeless body.

"Come on, Pette, wake up for Mama!" she cried out.

"You two must be there for one another. She needs you, and you need her," the sweet voice advised.

Scared to lay eyes on a body I vowed not to see, I listened to her words and went in behind Ms. Leeann.

My jittery hand that attempted to touch her back was rejected with bolts of despair. I couldn't do it. I tried my best. I bolted out the door past each.

"Dez, wait!" Past legs, trying to keep up with my brittle ones.

I ran, ran, ran down the stairs to the nearest door. Out behind the doors of hell, I escaped. There, the sunlight awaited me.

I cursed it! "How dare you! Your rays of beauty belong anywhere else but here!"

I searched for my car. Nothing. To a curb I approached. Traffic isn't steady enough to meet Lavarius right where he is.

"Fuck!" I cursed.

I collapsed in the grass, trying to calm myself. I wept, alone and afraid. Not afraid of tomorrow, but my very next breath.

"What do I tell my boys? Ohhh God. Ahkhim! What do I tell him? That man was his everything. How will the missing puzzle fit in when he is discarded permanently? I needed my Granny, but she was gone. I needed my Mommy, my Daddy, my TT, my Sister, my Brother, my Bestie, someone who loved me! But, they were all over 1000 miles away." I had to speak to someone.

Calling my Mommy. She instantly prayed for me, calling my Daddy, which sent him into an anxiety attack that bounced right back on me. There I lay, bargaining with death, talking to God, asking for strength. Strength to get up, strength to accept my breath, strength to live. At that very moment, all I wanted to do was die.

I slept to the lyrics running rapidly in my head, *"I don't wanna cry, but you know me so well. I just wanna hold back, but the tears keep coming. You may not love me now! But at least you loved me then!* Lavarius, you've just left me broken!" Awaken from my sleep.

What seemed to have been days later was his mother calling, "Where are you?"

"Outside on the curve," I answered.

"Girl, what are you doing out there?" she asked.

"I had to go. I have to go. I'm leaving," I confessed.

"Now you know you can't leave. You got to sign this paperwork," she alerted.

"You can do everything, Ms. Leeann, it's okay, I promise." There came the Knots back in my throat.

"Girl, get in here!" her voice screamed in frustration.

No way was I going to add any discontentment to the heavy emotions she felt already, so in I went. Mind so full of the thoughts that overtook the other. Body so limp it seemed like years before I made it to the waiting room, and in I went.

"Girl, you know you can't go nowhere," Ms. Leeann chuckled.

Flopping onto the seat, I had no response, nothing to offer outside of my numbness. Silence filled the air. Till she broke it with a question.

"So Dez, you and Pette divorced?"

"No, Ma'am, it wasn't final," I answered.

"Shit," she spits out quickly.

Questioning herself about whether she had really spoken those words out loud. Her face gave empathy that I refuse to pick up. How dare I? That was his mother. I already picked my seat in whatever happens next. Which was far from the driver's position.

"Okay, Dez, you gone send Pette home?" she asked, frightened of my response.

"Of course," I uttered with no hesitation.

Tears filled her eyes with relief and gratitude. Grabbing her hand with a squeeze.

"I would never do anything like that. I love you."

Paperwork arrived, and with a shaky hand, I scribbled my name, "Desiray Felton-Davis."

Before we parted ways. We agreed to meet at the place where Lavarius lived. The boys are still at home, unaware their world has just crumbled within 24 hours. Fear of looking at the boys made me take a detour home. Going to my friend's house, looking for something, only rewarded me with an empty release. The fear of facing the boys mocked me; I couldn't do it. His mother loved me, so she went to pick up the boys. They waited on me as I took my slow, sweet time destroying the world we built. Pappi was just 13, Jaylon was 11, Aiden was 8 years old, and baby boy was just five years old. I took my time and escaped. Drinking patron, patron, and more patron. This wasn't real. I'd wake up soon. So on to Mr. Vaugh's house I went.

PART TWO

This Too Shall Pass

"I've achieved so much in life

But my emotions are bankrupt

My body is nice and strong

But my heart is in a million pieces

When the sun is shining so am I

But when night falls, so do my tears

But then I hear a whisper that this too shall pass

-India Arie-

P ulling into the driveway, I took another sip of courage in the form of poison. It made life livable because it numbed it! I reached to turn off the ignition, then a song I had never heard blared through my speakers, pulsing tears I had hoped the patron swallowed!

"In the blink of an eye, just a whisper of smoke

You could lose everything, the truth is you never know

So I'll kiss you longer, Baby (Hey), any chance that I get

I'll make the most of the minutes and love with no regret

Let's take our time to say what we want (say what we want)

Use what we got before it's all gone (all gone)

'Cause no (no), we're not promised tomorrow"

-Megan Trainor and John Legend-

****

My heart broke all over again with the reminder. We're not promised tomorrow, or our very next breath. It was time for me to face the dreadful music awaiting behind those doors. There was no time for tears. I had to be there for these boys. So in I went.

Walking into the house, the stench of grief kissed my nostrils. My eyes located the boys. But they were bogged down with the flow of tears falling silently, too heavy to lift their heads and notice my transparent presence.

"We told them!" Voices in unison squealed out.

A betrayal of relief flushed over me. Yet, I rushed to comfort the boys, facing one of my worst nightmares. We sat there, no words falling from our lips. Just the hurt that screamed in rage from our beings. A sad symphony playing for us all to weep to. Snatching our minds back to reality. Out came Lavarius' belongings; they pulled them off him. We watched in silence as she skimmed through each piece. She towed out all that resided in his wallet, then emptied it into my hand. Twenty-two dollars and money cards shifted my mind to his words.

"My Wife told me to never leave the house without money in my pocket. So I got money, Bro. How much is a different story." He'd joke with anyone calling him broke with a laugh. Man, I missed that laugh!

"Dez!" Ms. Leeann called. Shifting my attention back to her eyes, tears of despair met mine.

"Can I have his wallet?" she whispered, holding back the floodgates that were ready to be broken again.

"You can have anything you want," I answered boldly.

I meant every word. I had no intention of driving this bus. My life was already in shambles. I wouldn't dare take on any of these tasks. Granny had finally been taken off life support per the doctor's orders. Telling them what I had been wailing about for the longest.

Granny was gone. No brain activity. Just machines keeping her at a place she didn't want to be. When I got word Granny had woken up chaotically, pulling out the wires, keeping her hostage, I lost my cool. I ended up separated from the very family I needed at this time! It's funny how we all wanted someone to blame for comfort. But in reality. Things were just the way they were because it was just the way it was. There was now another funeral that needed to be planned. They needed me to come and be present; I needed them to come to Texas and be present. But, hell, I checked out way back when.

There I sat, numb. Just there for the ride, I had been subpoenaed for. Everything that passed through me for approval was an automatic yes! I had absolutely nothing to offer, and they had nothing to give!

****

Outside, I stood, the sun no longer showed its face upon me. It knew better. I'd take the clouds and rain any day to reflect my heart. I could relate to that. I alerted the World of their Superman's forced retirement, never to return. Lots of messages, calls, and texts. Nothing that interested me. I needed a hug over and over again. I quickly snapped out of that desire! Reminding myself that no one owes me anything. Folks have their own lives. Their own trials and tribulations. I wouldn't dare add on to their load of burdens. So I didn't! I refuse to squander his funds left behind in his wallet. So I gave each relative in my presence a dollar to hold on to from their Petty-Witty! I took the last seven, 3 for me, my lucky number, and one for each of the boys! We'd frame it and have it forever! Each took their gift and returned a smile of gratitude. That's exactly the reaction Lavarius would have appreciated. I did the same.

Ms. Leeann and the crew loaded up what was left of Lavarius' belongings. Headed back to Arkansas. My eyes sank in, and my voice was timid.

"Ms. Leeann, there is nothing left for us in this place; the boys and I are going to move," I squealed out with unidentified conviction.

"Where you going?" she questioned.

"I'm not sure, maybe closer to Houston," I said.

"Okay, cool, my brother lives that way, so that's good."

"Okay! Drive safe. We love y'all," I said.

I sent them away with weld up eyes and a smile I tried to grow, but it wilted.

"See you soon!" I called out to the red GMC as it faded with the knots growing in my throat.

Call from "Red Bone."

A call from Lavarius' phone caught me off guard. When his father went to the location of heartbreak, he found it with a few other items.

"Hello," I answered.

A sweet voice echoed mine, "Hello," it was her! Lavarius Girlfriend.

I had to let her know what had happened. She had nothing to do with anything.

So I told her, "I'm so sorry, Honey! Lavarius passed away due to a car accident." Into shock, she went as I reminded her to breathe in and out like a snake.

"I just let him meet my daughter. I met his oldest son, and we were getting to know each other. 64 days of us bonding and then this?"

I listened to her go on and on. I suppose she loved him, but she didn't know him. She had no idea who my Black Country Superman was! She was just a placeholder, collateral damage. Yet, I comforted her on the phone as she counted days the same as I!

"I am so sorry, he told me you guys were divorced; we were working on his codependent issues. I told him..."

"Listen!" I interjected in between her rants, cries, and screams, "You owe me nothing, okay? You don't know me from a can of paint, and I don't know you from one. Lavarius and I were on our way to divorce, he was doing his own thing, and so was I!" I confirmed.

"I can send you money. Do you guys need anything?" she continued.

I overlooked her question, then spoke with all the sincerity I had for her.

"The funeral is next week, feel free to come and say a few words."

"God bless you, Honey!"

Before she could utter anything past a thank you. I ended the call. I had nothing to extend her! All that I had left in me belonged to my four boys! So, I marched right in to give it to them.

****

I couldn't tell you the last time I ate, I guess it showed because food was all they talked about.

"Dez, you hungry?"

"Dez, what you eat today?"

"Dez, take care of yourself!"

I gave lots of yes, Sirs, and yes, Madams to pacify them. I knew they were right; I heard them loud and clear.

"Take care of yourself, Ms. Rita!" I told myself that constantly; I just didn't know how to do that anymore.

Pulling up to our house, I glanced at the boys. Once separated, now together again by default. They were starving for their void to be filled.

"How the hell are you going to fill theirs when you're still searching for answers on how to regain your own sanity?"

As much as the children I took care of poured into me, I took off from work for at least a week. I had to go clean out Lavarius's truck. Which meant I needed a little bit more than my babies could offer.

I returned the boys to their distraction of TV and video games as mine walked through the door. No empathy or remorse intact. While numbness and I became one. This was a horrible nightmare I hadn't woken up from, right? Or was it? Did I even feel sad? Angry? Confused? Frustrated? No! I felt nothing at that moment. So much so, I put the boys to bed and went to a Blues concert to continue with my day! I danced all night long, becoming one with the music! It ended far too fast! Before I could utter my goodbyes, I dropped off my friend. I ran to meet the toilet, calling on Earl as my insides came tumbling out of me. Relinquishing my internal thoughts, out came bombs of smoke, clearing up any misunderstandings. A drunken tongue never lies, right?

"Oh, I love you, Lavarius, Fuck Me! I want you and only you!"

Some kind of truth rolled off my tongue as I enjoyed my playful ride.

By the time my friend stopped to question such bombs, it was too late to comfort me. The thick smoke coming from them choked me out to sleep. I went.

****

The birds composed such a magnificent piece to alert me of mourning. Opening my eyes, I saw Lavarius's canvas splattered on my wall!

"Good morning, Superman, I'm going to clean out that old, raggedy truck of yours today," I whispered.

Although the birds sang about peace and happiness, I felt empty. With the boys visiting their Pa Pa, I wondered if that was the reason why. Up and at it I went to the tow yard. Then, to get my boys was the mission, so that I could find out! So much for being a backseat rider; it was time for me to hop in the driver's seat. I mean, who else was going to? I pulled up to the tow yard, signed in, and waited patiently for my name to be called.

"Desiray Felton-Davis," an old, White, puny guy appeared before me.

"Yes, Sir," I called out.

"Follow me," he demanded.

Behind him, I walked for what seemed to be hours. He couldn't pick up the past any faster.

"I'm moving a bit slow today, my knees aren't the greatest!" he called out to me.

I said nothing. Focused on breathing long enough to make it to the truck that was under construction. The truck that kept him alive long enough for me to hear his heartbeat warmed my eardrums.

"There it is," he coughed.

He reached into his pocket for a tissue. My manners went out the window. I really meant to ask him if he was ok, if he needed me to run and get someone. But the imagery I stood gazing at froze me in place! It was burnt! It was crushed! Windows were missing! I instantly fell to my knees.

"Oh God! He suffered so much!" I cried out!

Weeping while grabbing his car club vest that hung out the door, I opened it. He held that car club tight! It was his family! His vest was no longer candy apple red. No longer did his patches stand out, which represented him. Country Boy, gone! Best Dad ever, gone! I am my brother's keeper, gone!

"What happened to you?" I questioned. Expecting an answer.

"I am so sorry, Lavarius, I'm so sorry!"

I held his vest tight and pleaded for his forgiveness! Hands latched onto my arms brought me to my feet! It was Mr. Vaugh!

"I knew you shouldn't come out here alone, Sweetie." Lifting me up into his truck, where his brother sat, didn't calm me.

"I'm so sorry, Lavarius," was all that fell from my lips

.Mr. Jimmy issued reassurance, attempting to settle the uproar my body had entered.

"Pette loved you, Dez. Regardless of what y'all had going on. Know that, Ok! None of this is on you. God makes no mistakes. Ok?" I answered with a nod.

In jumped Mr. Vaugh with a few other prized possessions. "I asked the guy to borrow some tools and took Pette's train horn out! I figure when the boys get older, one of them may want it!" he said. I gave another nod before drifting off to rest! I needed to reset for these boys, I was on my way to get.

****

Their voices announced our arrival. I woke up, looked out the window for confirmation, and there were my boys. Their outlines of what I once knew to be vibrant and bold now looked transparent. I see them in full capacity in a small glimpse.

"*Time to get your shit together, Ms. Rita,*" I told myself! "*Breath in, and out like a snake!*"

I listened to my legendary words passed down to the children! Out I jumped to hug them all with a vow that everything would be okay! Even if it wasn't, it would be!

If I knew how to do anything in this world, it was to be strong. I suppose that was the problem! I spent so much time being strong that I left no room for me to be truly happy. Just enough to get on by!

"*Smile and bear Dezy, smile and bear,*" I told myself.

****

Driving to Arkansas with the boys was a task I wasn't quite ready for. Lavarius was the one who drove us back down Highway 20. Now, for the first time in 10 years, it was all on me.

"*Keep me in your mirror, but don't take your eyes off the road. Holding on won't get us any nearer because we have a long way to go. Sometimes it's hard to see that somethings just can't be!*" -Madison Ryan Ward--sung out to me.

Her lyrics poking at my emotions filled my eyes. I looked to ensure the coast was clear before I gave them authorization to fall without disruption. Slightly sobbing without a definite reason why. I just wanted to be free. Free to be myself, but who was she?

Siri yelled, "Call from Ms. Leeann!"

The boys jumped awake, and I quickly cleaned my face. Then placed my smile in its proper place.

"Yes, Ma'am," I answered.

"How are y'all doing?" she asked."

"Girl, you know I don't do this driving mess. I need some Kool-Aid hell." We laughed together.

"Girl, you are showing out now?"

I loved her motherly tone towards me. I always loved the care she showed. I learned so much from her.

"Listen," she called out, "You may need to pull over, we're finalizing Pette's service arrangements." She included me in everything.

I was grateful, but ultimately, I wanted whatever she wanted. Being the wife meant I was legally in charge of driving this bus. Fortunately, she and I had an unspoken agreement that she really was! Well, it's what I hoped, but reality was just that. Real life!

Finally, we arrived at our destination six hours later by the grace of God. We pulled up to the house where Lavarius was born, and the place where he took me to meet his mother. The very first place I fell in love with the country.

Boom! There was that brother-in-law. The one who swore I tried to kill him. But there he was, very much alive. The sound of the door latches locking sent the boys back to the car. Ms. Leeann was at work, yet welcomed us to come to the house as we always do. We were just going to be there till our room was ready. However, access denied! I looked him in his eyes as he escaped our company!

His eyes looked back and yelled! "You killed my brother!"

Again, it screamed through his bloodshot pupils. Ensuring I heard the first time! The guilt I buried in the pits of nonexistence started to make its debut. I had to leave the boy's sight. Off I went through the fields, and I walked to his grandmother's house. I allowed the overflow of tears to be reasoned with.

"Stop it, Girl, no tears. You left because it was time for you to go! The Lord instructed you to do just as you did!" I told myself.

"Did I believe my leaving played a big part in his death? Had we been together that night, or even if I had been in his ear instead of his music? Would things be different? Maybe the boys would still have the only thing in this world that kept them steady. Lavarius was their Daddy! Their entire world had just been torn away from them.

So, when his eyes reminded. "You killed Pette." I believed him.

But I had no time for tears. Mama would have torn me a new tail had I walked in there with a droopy face! I got myself together, and in I walked with a knock!

"Hey, Ms. Crisa Lee," I exclaimed with joy.

"Hey, Baby, come on in, sit down," she insisted.

Her words always seemed to cut as I listened yet demanded my earlobes to shut to avoid further bleeding. It was nothing new. Lavarius told me how his grandmother was way back when. If I were coming to see her, it meant

I welcomed insults to injury. I was grateful the visit flew by. It was time to say goodbye, so I stood in anticipation of the relay of mockery of my halting. Instead, she said, sensing my displeased energy.

"I done got too old to care about what I say. Hell, I figure if I'm thinking it, I may as well say it. Cuz what can you do?"

In my mind, I answered: *"If I were driving this bus, I could do a lot."* Instead, I said, "Okay then, our room is ready, we will see you before we pull out."

"Alright then, y'all be safe!" she said, shutting the door behind me.

Words of distraught discombobulated me. She called me a sorry wife. Maybe I was. I hated feeling anything. I'd end up falling into the grave I dug years ago, waiting on standby for me to fall in. The boys needed me to be their rock, to keep them afloat. So that's what I did.

****

My Auntie flew in from Georgia to be in my corner. I had no one else. She flew into Texas, then drove to Arkansas with my nonprofit friends. I welcome them with open arms and gratitude for their presence and help. The boys were gifted brand new tuxedos and shoes. Folks sent us food every night, and it felt marvelous to have unsolicited help.

I always said, "If you see a need and can fill it, fill it. End of story!"

We pulled up to their small-town funeral home, and my nerves went bananas. Being gifted a drink of Kool-Aid from Ms. Leeann made me calm enough to go inside, where his body resided. In waiting for the paperwork, my trembling hands misconstrued the signature on it. It was the fact that we now had to do a closed casket because of all the swelling he had endured. It sent my mind to the edge of what the fuck is this. Anxiety about a funeral I was going to be front and center at. Adamant about sharing a poem I wrote was only part of the nightmare I swore this was.

Dear Superman
(That name I gave you stuck, huh?)

After Hundreds and Hundreds
Of Excess Pains.
My Heavenly Father Instructed.
FOLLOW ME and reap ALL the desires of your Heart.
Whether you're on Earth or in Heaven
We Love Each Other
So, we will NEVER BE APART

We were drenched in Tons of Rain.
But let NO ONE CONFUSE that with
Tons of Pain.

We experienced the Good, Bad, and Ugly
Of Each Other.
Memories NO ONE
Can take from us.

We were Blooming Flowers

Weathering the Storm, Sleet and Snow

We took a Break to Grow

Then, Boom left for good!

That's why it's So Damn Hard

TO LET YOU GO!

I vow to stay Humble and Consistent.

As You Guide the boys on their Journey.

I'll remind them to Slow Down.

Being sure NOT to Live Life in such a hurry.

Our God is an AWESOME GOD

Who SITS High and Looks Low

This was His Plan when He Says YES

NO ONE ELSE CAN SAY NO!

Not even us!

I've accepted that this Plan is Out of My Hands

Please Catch My Kiss in Heaven

My Black Country

SUPERMAN!

Funeral cars pulled up. I stood still. Feet frozen to the ground. *"Come on, wake up, Dezarita!"* I barked at myself while pinching my arm for assistance.

"Come on, Dezy!" Swooped my Auntie, grabbing my hand, then grabbing Ahkhim's.

She directed me to the first hearse, where the doors were opened by the driver, offering his condolences. Scooting my old white dress across the seat, I looked around.

"So, this is what the inside of one of these things looks like," I thought as eyes looked at me crazy.

I guess this was just my first funeral I was a part of. I didn't go to these kinds of things. I didn't believe in them.

"Cremate my ass, skip the funeral and pour me over water somewhere beautiful."

I'd always tease Lavarius with my death wishes. He let it go in one ear and out the other. Granny didn't like all that fuss either. Yet, over 1,000 miles away, they were planning hers. I wanted to be there to ease my Daddy's pain, my sisters, my T-tees, brothers, hell, all of them. But who did I think I was? My superwoman cape no longer fits. I had given the boys all I had to supplement such empty cups. I had nothing left for anyone, not even myself!

Walking into the service behind Ms. Leeann with the boys sent my knees reflexes into motion. There, his face lit up all over. Lawd, knows I just needed to make it to the front pew. My knees getting weak pushed a little more pep in my step. I speed up. Finally taking my seat, I glanced around the church! Then heard a voice scream loudly in my ear!

"Dub up or shut up!" Apparently, I was the only one who did.

The Car Club sat still, quiet, in mourning. That had to have been Lavarius in my ear. He was reminding me that the folks I called side pieces, and no-good dirty jokers, showed up like the family he called them. Each life he touched showed up to pay their respects. The clout I swore they chased was at a standstill for this moment. Big Country's Farewell. Such a beautiful service it was. I suppose I could say we did that. But was I really driving this bus?

****

It was ironic how Lavarius had just passed his probationary period the week of the car wreck. That granted him full benefits. Honey, I called his workhouse and did all the legwork to get that paper trail in order. When his job paid for his service in full, I shouted in gratitude. Tell me that isn't God! How about our divorce would have been final that next week? Yet, it was voided due to our no-call no-show. He had no time to label his beneficiary, so by default, it all went to me! His wife! However, I knew his mother was always on his paperwork as one. He just hadn't had the time to add her. I never objected then, so I wasn't going to start now. Half the funds were allocated to her after I set the boys' trust fund up. I had no second guesses about it! It was the right thing to do. Yet, the daggers I received had me questioning my existence. I gave everyone I held near and dear something. That wasn't enough. They say money is the root of all evil! It's an explanation the Lord gives of greed! I saw it firsthand! It was sickening to see his death be a deliberation! Pumping everyone's behavior back into its normal rhythm. The air between them and me turned cold when they didn't receive what they wanted from me! Now, the few folks that I had in my corner talked amongst each other. Finding out I issue rewards $2.00 more than the other. I did what I knew how to do. I clung onto my friend. At least I knew the way she felt about me. It was no secret.

They say, "Something is better than nothing."

I suppose I felt that bad when it came to her. Still searching and waiting for a void to be filled! Unfortunately, it was as hollow as an old oak tree! But, still, I took what I could get! I understood that sometimes the things we needed from folks were just needs they genuinely couldn't fill! So, no love lost, no love gained.

****

Cars blasting music, doing donuts, popping willies, and doing stunts. I know Lavarius was smiling down in Heaven. All the excitement reminded me we were back in Texas, where everything was bigger and better! The boys yelled, cheering on the cars!

"It's a parade inside my city!" chanted Pappi, recording all the live action!

We rode to the spot that marked the beginning of our lives turned upside down! Balloons released, speeches made, loads of condolences passed to the family. Together, the City showed up all in remembrance of Big Country! It did my heart good to see the CEO of the car club place my baby boy on his shoulders.

The tears started to flow from Ahkhim as he spoke in that soft, timid voice, "I miss my daddy." Tears of helplessness came over me.

What else could I do to cease his heartache? To see him smile again. I've taken this little boy shopping, wrapped him in my arms as he broke time and time again. I just wanted him to smile again. But I guess he felt he had no reason to. I know I did!

I expressed my gratitude to all of them for such a wonderful day. Before I knew it, guilt came back to say hello, and I lost it. But the thing about this is, I had all of his side pieces there to catch me, and they did.

****

Restless but exhausted, I lay. I've never been the animal type, but I had gone out and bought myself a beautiful baby Doodle. Koda was my emotional support dog. He went with me everywhere. I'm not sure if I've been able to sleep if he didn't cuddle up beside me. But sometimes even he got sick of me and went to sleep at the other end of the bed, leaving me to wonder! I wondered if Lavarius knew exactly how I felt before he left this earth?

I wonder if he knew when the D Word

Became the Main Topic.

I MEANT NO HARM.

It was just me trying to get him to Transform

Into the man I KNEW he could be!

THAT WAS THE KEY!

I wonder, did he know?

When he Signed on the Dotted Line.

Yes,

I smiled in Agreement with His Choice

Thinking I was FINALLY taking Back My Voice.

Assuming such burdens would be Released from Me.

Yet, I ended up Being Buried

BY NEW ONES

Brick by Brick-by-Brick.

I wonder if he knew I wore his Shame and Pain.

As he offered Comfort Dipped in Chocolate.

Presented with a Persistent Bow.

Of course, I COULDN'T tell him NO.

Man, I wonder, did he know?

Did he know our boys NEEDED HIM as he…

Flatlined, Flatlined, and Flatlined

RIGHT BEFORE MY EYES?

Leaving me there ALONE STRANDED.

Unable to capture the Free Air

As I yelled out in disbelief.

OHH GOD, MY GOD THIS SHIT ISN'T FAIR!

Did he know as I kissed him

ONE LAST TIME?

His Soul Crossed Over

Then he was NO LONGER MINE?

I wonder if he knew when the words,

"FIGHT FOR YOUR BOYS!"

Raced off My Tongue.

I Meant Me Too.

Did he know that space was

What I asked for to Breathe

Not for him to

PERMANENTLY LEAVE?

If only he knew I'd sit out Watching Clips

On how THINGS used to be.

Blind to the Fact.

That I MUST Let Go and Let It Be.

So, I'll continue to wipe the Boy's Tears.

Reminding: HAVE NO FEAR

Your Daddy is ALWAYS NEAR.

I'll keep putting 1 Foot in Front of the Other.

Trying my best to be an Awesome Mother.

Creating new patterns as I Live Life

Remembering it's okay to Let Myself Cry.

As I reflect on the 10 YEARS we spent together

And Apart.

Smiles and Frowns.

Joy and Pain.

There it was.

THE CONFIRMATION FINALLY CAME.

Of Course, He Knew!

****

To sleep, I tried to fall with a heavy heart. Then the wails of celebration went off!

"Hey, Mr. Sexy Man! What your name is?"

Tiger Niles sang her blues loud through my phone, forcing me to pick it up.

"Happy birthday to my Mr. Sexy Man!" It read.

It was a reminder of Lavarius' birthday. I reached for the bottle of tequila instead of the cold plate of food I had collected as leftovers after making dinner for the boys. But it was empty. I had nothing else to turn to. So, I wrote.

The clock. Struck 12 and it became your birthday. What will I do today? I will wake up in good spirits, get cute just as I know you'd want me to. I'll take the boys to their destination and play all your jams. I bet your fat baby will demand me to turn them off. So, then I'll turn to our Blues and think of you. The other day. I talked to your mother on FaceTime. Seeing your grave site took me out. I suppose I was just faced with the reality! You're really gone. After looking at your grave site, night fell upon me quicker than it was supposed to! Back to bed, rot I went! I blame my fatigue on so much work. Watching the boys buy it as they missed the tears that fell right along with it. I miss you! You loved me! Like, really freaking loved me. Will that ever come again? Not like you, I bet! Even all the bad couldn't outweigh your love at the end of the day. You know, no one really understands how I feel, and that's OK. But I am so broken. I was once this way. Remember long ago how you helped me put the pieces back together again. You were indeed my Superman, flying to my rescue. Lavarius, I had an ounce of hope in me that I'd have you again. You heard me say I just need to heal, and if it's meant to be, it will be. Then boom, you are gone. Like really? I'm not sure if I'm ready to accept how I lost us then. I sure as hell can't say I am ready to accept how I lost you now. All I wanted was a fresh start for both of us, a new foundation. But you know how I roll. I regret nothing but having my switch turned off, which I naturally could not control. If only I had...

"Boom! Boom! Boom!" Noises from the bathroom put me on my feet! I pushed open the door to witness Pappi in rage. He stood punching the closet door! Releasing yelps of pain in the dark till I turned on the light. He had every right to be free. He had every right to feel how he needed to feel.

But tearing up things that did not belong to us was unacceptable! He froze and gathered himself. I stood there patiently, stunned by his performance.

Lost for words. "I'm sorry, Ma," he released in a sigh.

"I just felt like fighting someone, so I came to punch the door."

Disappointment poured out of his explanation. A nod is all I gave. The tears bubbled up in the crevices of my eyes. To avoid them breaking the rules, I quickly followed him back into his room while taking deep breaths.

"Breath in, and out like a snake," I told myself.

"Pappi, I understand you feel angry, upset, and frustrated. Just remember this is not our home, we must pay for these things when we leave," swallowing the knots in my throat, I spoke softly to him.

"Yes, Ma'am," he replied.

"Do you want to talk?" I asked, hoping for the answer to be no, because I was going to burst right then and there. Then my cover would be blown.

"I Miss L!" So afraid to speak his full name, trying to protect the other boys from hearing.

"I understand. We all do. Look, Bro, I'm here for you for anything and everything. Everything is going to be OK, I promise you. Now get back in bed and try to get some rest. We opened the daycare in the morning." I spoke.

"Yes, Ma'am," he whispered. We embraced, as I said, goodnight.

****

My friend and I collaborated on opening a daycare at her place. Her place was bigger, and my license was still restricted. We worked together, splitting the revenue 50/50. The rise in my income helped me gift the boys every distraction they asked for. Doing things just as their dad would. But at the end of the day, I wasn't him. Which is why the birth mothers of the boys I raised took them away. On one hand, there I was consulting a lawyer, fighting for my family.

The lawyer gave it to me straight: "In the state of Texas, you don't legally have rights unless you adopt. In your case, your rights died with your husband, who legally had all the rights."

She wished me luck and dropped my case. On the other hand, I had Ahkhim, who needed someone to blame. I fell victim to such! On his 6th birthday, I surprised him with VIP tickets to a huge Monster Truck Race. Although his dad was gone, he could still enjoy a passion they both shared, with their favorite meal, chicken and fries. Halfway through the show, he lost it. Tears could have drowned all the monster trucks. I didn't know what to do.

"OK, let's go home, Baby," I whispered.

Walking down the steps, he gave it to me. "It's all your fault!" he spat out.

"Wait, my fault?" I spoke in confusion.

To hear the frustration leave his mind and run off his tongue so quickly shocked me. No reply was returned. Just tears of what looked like a rainbow of emotions being released. I let him feel how he needed to feel, as a warm embrace fell over him from me. Still not quieting his pain. Pappi took his hand as they walked at Ahkhim's old man's pace. I let go of him to walk to the car in mine! "I'll meet y'all back at the car!" I shouted.

My emotions weren't going to be obedient much longer. I had to go release in the normal spurts I granted myself! I cried because the words were just a song that continued to play on repeat on my radio station!

Four weeks later, Pappi was now checked into an inpatient psychiatry hospital, taking antidepressants for attempting to take his own life.

"It was too much pressure, Ma!" he spoke out in front of the doctor after failing his mental health screening.

"What is Pappi?" I replied in embarrassment!

I asked him if he wanted to talk on numerous occasions. Why wouldn't he open up to me? I confirmed I was here for him. Now we're here at the doctor for his yearly physical, and he is telling me he tried to take his own life several times. Showing me marks for proof? Where was I? In the next room over, in the bed rotting? Out Ubering? Out trying to get another bottle to numb myself, or an empty release from my friend to hold me over?

"What the fuck!" I blurted out before I could stop the words from skipping off my tongue with their full intensity! On he went, breaking down a wall society helped him build!

"They said I needed to step up and be the man of the house now, to help you, to help my brothers. But I can't. Ahkhim keeps crying. You're losing weight. I miss Lavarius, too. We may not have been close, but I do! I was 4 when he came into my life. I just turned 13 yesterday. He taught me so much, and I just miss him. Like, why did you have to move away from him, Ma? Why did y'all have to separate anyway? I just miss him."

In my arms, he collapsed. I had no words. My tears hollered out all that needed to be said. The doctor's face was red and wet! What was she thinking? I feared the next step.

"Please don't let them take my Baby!"

But Pappi shut all that down as his 5'3", 132lb body collapsed in my arms! He buckled into the first position I held him in.

"What have I done? Ohhh God?" That was all I could say!

Grief, waiting to be grieved, all in different forms. The family we built 10 years ago was now in pieces I couldn't recognize, again. Brothers once together, now separated once more. Who was really driving this damn bus?

To my friend, I ran for whatever she could give me, tangible to feel right then and there. Truth is, if I kept the yeses coming: $10,000: check. Tummy Tuck: check. Trip to Miami for my birthday: check. Trip to the Bahamas for family vacation: check! She complied. I mean, wouldn't you? I wouldn't trip about anything. I paid to get what I needed to stay above ground. The proof was in the pudding. There I was. Still trucking along, fighting alongside my boys, living this thing called life!

Diary Entry:

"Today makes. Nine months since Lavarius has been gone. The boys have gone away to get a break in Arkansas, and I am just sitting here. Still tripping on the fact that we separated for growth. Then I went to file for divorce just to be done with it. Told him several times that if it's meant to be, we'd get back together and start fresh. I suppose I just don't understand God's doing now. I know for certain that my boys needed their dad. They need him now and will forever and always. I don't know why, but there is a disconnect in me somewhere. I miss him so much. Yet the consistent flow of tears seems to be locked up. They can't escape as they need to. I can't be weak. I must keep this facade up! I still can't believe Bianca didn't come save me this time. As much as I was there for her! She confirmed she didn't know how to be there for me. It was cool. I had made my peace with it! She owed me nothing! No one did!"

I wonder if my bestie, my siblings, or anyone I showed up for stayed away in doubt? Wondering what they could offer me. Hell, all they had to do was ask me again. I wouldn't say I was good this time! I knew now exactly what I needed! I needed a safe place to feel how I needed to feel! I needed to give the levy permission to break. Allow my rivers of despair to run rapidly. To clear out all in its way so that maybe I could be washed and renewed. But I couldn't! I had to keep rebuking our past that tried to hunt me and replace my emotions with resentment. I'm going to hang on to the memories of joy. To laughter. To fussing and fighting just because I wanted to. I want my Superman back. I want to grieve him wholeheartedly. I want my tears to flow as they wake up my being. Showing me what it means to really live as I used to.

-Signed: *Dashai-*

Six months of my life gone, wasted, but no regrets. We live, we learn, and we take losses with our chin up. I've been stuck in denial somewhere between depression, but through Christ I can do all things, and it was time to show it. I made up my mind that I was going to release and be free. I started separating myself from the life I once lived. I bought a house two hours away, where we were thankful to God for our fresh start. Back to Christ, I ran. *"Train up a child in the way that they will go and they will not depart." Proverbs 22:6.*

Why I tried to do it my way versus the Lord's way is beyond me. But I am rooted in Christ, so home is where I always return. My faith had always been rooted in Christ. It was just clogged with too many distractions to remember. Like the clips I received on Facebook. It was live footage of the Lavarius wreck. An X military lady happened to be driving past. I saw the accident and stopped to help.

Her message read, "I've been looking all over Facebook for you. I was with your husband up until the paramedics arrived. He was not alone!"

Instantly pressing play, I saw how the truck had been flipped over on its roof. How the glass had shattered in the mix of the rumbling, discharging his items from it and him to the very back of his trunk. He was such a big guy, tossed all over that vehicle. Ending up in such a tiny space, crunched up. I lost my composure!

"Can you hear me? I'm here to help. Open your eyes. Look at me. Stay with me," she said to him so sweetly.

Yearning to hear him respond, I held my breath. But all he gave were grunts.

"He is still alive; I'm going to try to pull him out," then the clip ended.

A new one has begun. "Hey, are you okay?" she opened the driver's door to a big black truck.

Blood covered his face, leaking from his head!

"Fuck, what did I hit?" I yelled at the phone.

"You hit my husband, you Dumb Bitch!" Anger took over me!

This is the guy who hit him. The drunk, the report showed, hit him, knocking him back into the cement barricade. The clip ended, forcing me to focus on the last clip. Paramedics covered the scene with cops. There they were with the jaws of life, cutting his "Chevy Heavy" apart to obtain his body. I noticed the engine burned in this clip just as it was in the tow yard. Just as his 1st sergeant's vest reflected. *"What happened out there?"* I flashback to my run-in with the Detective on his case. To the station I marched for some clarification. Receiving calls from lawyers who wanted to represent me. Had me questioning, how were they telling me my husband died because he was intoxicated? That was the very bar he was at, I could sue.

"He was at a bar?" I questioned, "I thought he was kicking it with his play sister!" I demanded answers! She gave me the report. I read it right then and there!

"Bullshit!" I shouted!

"Ma'am, this report says my husband is the suspect! It's written as if he committed suicide," I said with a neck roll, ready for whatever.

"There has been a new detective assigned to your case. However, she isn't in today! They are still investigating," she said.

"But this says final report! This is public records, and it's a lie. I need it fixed expeditiously!"

An officer came from around the desk! Black muscles looked as if they were going to jump out of his uniform to choke me up. His spectacular smile should have calmed me, the way his teeth sparkled, but it didn't!

"Calm down, Ma'am," he warned.

"I'll calm down when somebody fix this, because like I said: Bull-Fucking-Shit!"

"What was wrong with me? Did I forget I was at the jailhouse? That

all he had to do was pick my 92-pound stiff bones up and toss me in a cage."
Truth is, I didn't care.

As my Auntie Bernice says, "Once you take me there, it's hard for me to come back. So just let me be!" He grabbed my hand, pulling me out of the sight of the other officers who were ready to lock me up.

"Listen, Honey, I understand you are grieving, but you can't be acting like this at a police station. Here is the Chiefs' number. Give him a call, he will fix everything." I took the card, looked at him, and walked away.

Immediately calling to leave a message on his voicemail. Two days later, the report was fixed! Closing his case with the cause of death due to blunt injuries! Everything is public records these days. Which is why I went so hard to capture the truth! I'll be damned if my boys had to look at any records with their dad on it and see suicide. I wouldn't let anything or anyone taunt their memory of him! Not even me!

The clips confirmed all of that. So maybe it wasn't a distraction after all. It was the start of my closure, knowing he wasn't alone, jumpstarting my healing! Here goes nothing!

PART THREE

Healing

"I release all disappointments

From my Mental, Physical, Spiritual, and Emotional Bodies

'Cause I know that Spirit guides me

And love lives inside me

That's why, today I take life as it comes!"

-India Arie-

My phone turned into a Decorative Piece

On My Nightstand.

What was the point? I was over it.

As I wallowed underneath My Burdens--

The Phone Rang!

Now, as much as you know

How I ISOLATE from the world.

When Mine is a Mess...

The Buzzing Continues!

So you'd like me to talk to you?

"Come on and Vent, Ms. Rita."

I'M HERE FOR YOU!

Please don't get Me Wrong, Boo.

I'm EXTREMELY grateful

Just Curious to know

What EXACTLY does that do for you?

You desire My Bricks to be

STACKED upon yours?

Break You Down

So you can later Blame Me for your Frown?

Or would you rather

Have Me Cry and Yell

WISH ME WELL

As you exclaim

"Just Pray About It?"

Please!

Do tell!

Okay Boom:

I hadn't had An Appetite in days

Because my fragile body is Full of Emotions

LIKE RAGE!

No Fury!

No Fuckin' Fear!

So what then?

Oh, let me NOT FORGET

Alcohol is ALL My Taste Buds long for

I NEED IT to Numb My Pain

I ADORE how it Dry's My Rain!

Oh Yeah

Sleep is as far...

As You Are from Me!

So why in the Hell CAN'T YOU SEE...

When I REQUIRED your presence

You were as invisible as the Pain I Feel

Forcing Me to Figure Out

A way to Constantly Heal!

When I Subpoenaed your Voice

Your ACTIONS highlighted your Choice!

It's why I Solemnly Swear to Choke

On Each Thirst of Help

I would RATHER Weep Silently!

And Shrug My Shoulders

With a Welp!

Let me ask you something?

Do you have a Guilt Trip Setting In?

Are you now Drawn to Clean Up

My world and Make Me Whole Again?

Are you interested in now Becoming My Friend?

How so?

Do I lend My Burdens to you for you to

Routinely dump them

ALL Back On Me.

Reveal my decreased weight.

For you to Make Jokes

Laugh

And Hide Your Plate?

Do I drink my drink like it's Tea

Just for me to become the Main Topic

As You ALL SECRETLY Judge Me.

Out of Sight

Out of Mind

Will be My Go-To

EVERY DAMN TIME!

I Am Sorry!

A Call or Text JUST WON'T DO!

Show me your Love by Showing Up To

Wrap Me in Your Arms!

RECIPROCATION IS KEY!

So Bro!

Make that Shit Make Sense

Or Please!

DON'T COME BOTHERING ME!

What was I thinking! They didn't let me be! Every other week, I was the casualty of a wellness check. So I knew they cared. I was in my healing era. Asking for help was one of my assignments from my psychiatrist.

"In that case, why don't y'all get this teenager of mine so I can reconnect with this lil boy of mine?" I asked, and I received a yes!

Pappi had gone to Green Bay, WI, for the 8th grade! He had an entire support system there! I had built Ahkhim and I one here! Look at God!

It was the first year in our newly owned house! I would no longer be Ms. Dezy! I understood his Daddy was his world. I understood he mimicked what he heard daycare kids call me. I understood there was a disconnect between us. Since birth, our bond was taunted. But I would change that. I am his mother. He is my son. His Dad may be gone, and I am so sorry he is! What we had to understand was that I was not!

Each morning, I made breakfast, walked him to 1st grade, and walked to pick him up. We talked daily. Did homework. We bonded. He enjoyed learning, just as I enjoyed teaching him five years ago with my childcare kids. Sports and dancing became a part of our lives. No more distractions. Just therapy with pictures that were drawn for expressions when he couldn't talk. Smiles were starting to be snuck in with embraces. He started to heal right along with me. We sat out under the moonlight, enjoying nature.

"Look, that's my daddy, he is a star now," he said, "You're right about that, Baby Boy." I smiled back.

We had made this all a habit. Each night, I'd remind him, "I love you and I'm here for you."

Still more tears came, more nightmares came, and more anger directed at me came. The "I miss and want my Daddy" never left. But I stayed steady. Determined is an understatement when it came to him!

"I love you and I'll always be here for you," I'd say to him.

"One night," he answered back, "I love you too, Mommy!" I cried in awe before I jumped for joy!

"Boom, we got action!" I celebrated.

****

Conversations with my friend faded out. There was nothing there but unresolved animosity. Truth is, I'd still be there! I'd still be there if I announced myself as bruised, beaten down, and broken.

Maybe then you'd be able to Declare
MY NEEDS as Wants, and My Fears...

Fake then simply plan your Escape
I'd still be there if we followed Our Mind
VERSUS Our Hearts
Without stepping in, as Nature did its Part.

Were the Feelings Felt on our part False
RATHER than True
Were they Based Off Impulse?

Did it feel SO DAMN GOOD
That the Facts of Should a Could a Would a
Were pushed into Space,
Floating Meaningless
To be GRABBED on Another Date?

Actually, I'd Still Be There

If the Fragments My Mind held

Didn't create their Own Scenarios.

Worried if you Would Stay, or if I Should Go.

Mesmerized by the Connection Caused

By Fake Affection,

I pushed you AWAY for Protection.

If I knew grief would make me Fall Apart.

So easily taking ALL my cares with me

Getting attached to the hand that Lifted Me

I'd have done things Differently

Well, Yes, it was good for you

Cause My Flaws were Thrown in My Face

Out of the Blue.

Yes, I SAW your heart.

Which is why I EXPECTED you to Depart.

Reassurance was the Key

To My Double-Sided Mind!

Confirmations that I Could Be Myself,

ALL THE TIME

I wish I were Granted Grace!

A moment to Find Balance after a while.

Truth is,

You just DIDN'T want to Give the Time.

I should have HANDLED My Mind, Body, and Soul

With Care

Instead, I FUMBLED them ALL

So Close to Death.

All because I Couldn't Care.

I'D STILL BE THERE.

If you TRULY WANTED me to be.

I'd STILL be there

If I didn't ALLOW myself to Believe this was

Just a Ride Waiting to End.

Welp!

That's that!

On that, because I AM GONE LIKE THE WIND

SO I REST MY PAPER AND PEN!

I wanted it to be known that if I was still stuck in my own shit! I could have easily gone back to enter our toxic cycle! I, trying to make a point, left the door open for her toxicity. It followed me to Corsicana! She went on my social media to enroll me in cyberbullying! I was every name but the child of God! She wanted the world to know I didn't care about my husband's death! How I didn't even grieve him! But instead, I went to a concert the same day! It hurt me! She was right! I didn't grieve Lavarius! But that all was about to change!

I said my hateful words to her, throwing her belongings in a fire as I cried and wrote to release! Forgiveness was my friend! Granny said it best, "If someone sees a fool, they'll bump their head!" I was that fool amid our transaction! But no more!

A Letter to My Friend:

I often reflect.

Forgive!

Then Forgive More.

What a Transaction Orchestrated by God.

Carried Out by the Merchant:

You

Customer:

Me!

Dreadful moments of services

Paid in Full Rise.

I Push Past them all.

Retaliation after the fact,

Deemed me all the above in your Leisure.

Again, I Pushed Past them all.

Throwing them into the Sea of Forgiveness

Then watched as they Submerged.

How my smile sparkled as I Sat in Solitude.

Trying to bring back my Joyful Tune

The receipt of Our Transactions

Wasn't labeled NULL AND VOID.

It was APPROVED with the Misconstrued

Definition of Life's Examples of Love,

Lust and Luxury, JUST TO LIVE!

Life Lessons Documented

As its charge that I'm STILL Paying For!

A Transaction Orchestrated by God.

Carried Out by the Merchant:

YOU

Customer:

ME.

Marked complete with a CHECK MARK of Forgiveness

In the leisure of Our Hearts.

That Transaction, Orchestrated by God,

Stained History: The Study of Past Events.

Yet, relevant in Our Lives Each Day.

Forgiveness is the KEY that Sets Souls Free.

Maybe that explains why I've Flown Beyond

Where ANY Naked Eye Can See.

I Forgive You and I Love You.

I wish you NOTHING but the Best.

Goodbye, and Take Care of Yourself.

Love, Ms. Dez

****

It's funny, you know, the very thing I wanted Lavarius to do, what I longed for him to deliver while he was alive and well on this earth, he was doing from the Heavens up above! He made it so I didn't have to work. I took advantage of it while I focused on grieving him and healing. Not just his death, but issues I swept under the rug, were now peaking from underneath. I was on a mission to become a healthier me.

After I walked baby boy to school, I went to the Y. I meditated and participated in yoga. Learned health and Wellness techniques that helped me to slowly wean myself off liquor all day, every day, and eat. I picked up a pen instead, stepping back into my creative flow! I danced out my emotions. I wrote out my emotions. But most of all, I cried out my emotions. They no longer filled me.

Aware that nothing happens overnight! I realized I had a long way to go. So I stayed Solo-Dolo in the country, healing! I asked for nothing! God had blessed me far more than I could have imagined! Yet, I still cried myself to sleep, desiring to erase just one more memory!

If I could ERASE One More Memory.
It would be ALL the
Pain and Agony we went through.

The Slow Sufferings that pierced my heart, Full of Love.

Leaking uncertainty onto My Physical Being.
So much so that I struggled to Recognize
The reflection Staring Back at Me.

I just want my mind to Dance Around
The Spontaneous Nights
Full of Laughter
OVER ABSOLUTELY NOTHING.

Can I bask in the fight

You Won with My Heart?

Cry Tears of Joy as I remember on loop

The way you freed My Broken Heart

From the Castle of Despair,

I held Myself Hostage In.

Let Me Dream with Smiles

NOT BE a product of My Fears.

Can I just Dance to our song of Gratitude

We SANG OUT on top of each steep hill.

Not the Rain, Sleet, and Snow

We hiked in to Get There.

If I could ERASE One Memory,

It would be the fact that I LOST YOU AT ALL.

Then. Now. Forever.

GONE TOO SOON, MY SUPERMAN.

But I rest in Our Wonderful Memories, as I know.

I SHALL SEE YOU AGAIN!

-Love your Dashai'-

P.S. I suppose I should be saying...

Lord CONTINUE to take My Pain Away

Replacing it with Your Purpose

OVER MY LIFE!

Consistently Providing Peace

That Passes All Understanding!

Lord help me be Content

IN EVERY CIRCUMSTANCE.

As I Re-Claim

JIRAH!

YOU ARE ENOUGH!

****

Yes Lord! You are enough! I Thanked God! We had made it thus far. It marked the end of a dreadful year! Pappi was still in Green Bay playing basketball and running track. I was proud of how much he had healed with the help of his outlets. He broke a 1972 record at the middle school in track. I was amazed thinking. It took sending him 1000 miles away for him to want to play sports versus sitting in the house watching that game. However, I took my wins where I could. As I decided we were going to surprise him for his last basketball game!

I swore I'd stay away from Green Bay. My granny had been taken abruptly, so what else lay there for me? I thought. Can I go through with this? Go all the way to Green Bay and know that she isn't there, not be able to see her? I questioned myself in search of a command to abort this mission. But all I got was an urge to go find out.

Ahkhim and I flew up to Green Bay in the cold Winter months. We surprised him for his last basketball game, receiving bolted runs to my arms, screaming my name when he realized I was at his school, 1000 miles away from Texas. I'd do anything for them. I hope he knew that.

Back in our room, the boys enjoyed each other. That little boy really missed his Big Brother. They were inseparable. I went out on the town. Solo-dolo indeed Ubering wherever I wanted to go. I deserved it. Passing my granny's old place caused my heart to race in an unexplainable way. Reaching my destination.

"We're here, Ma'am." I sat there, unable to move as quickly as I desired.

"Yes, Sir," I spoke, exiting the car and walking into the lounge.

From the moment I opened the door, the loud music faded as I walked in. The people dancing disappeared. There I stood in this dark hole spinning, as my heartbeat became the new DJ.

My bestie was right there in arm's reach, but I couldn't call her. Reflecting on our visit yesterday frightened me! I unloaded my healing journey on her. So excited to be in a safe place, I ran my mouth as fast as it could go! It took her for a loop. Same old, same old with me. I could be stuck in a hole, but I wouldn't dare pick up the phone to let anyone know I was drowning! She was right, she wasn't just anyone. She has been my best friend since the 9th grade. Well over 15 years of history. She needed me to pick up that phone, text her, and keep her updated on my life so she can be there for me. In my reality, I didn't know how to do that. Figuring things out on my own had been ingrained in me. A phone call wasn't enough for me. I didn't want it. I needed her in Texas with me! Where was she ALL those times I needed her to hug me, to reassure me as I shed my humility on her shoulders, proving I was no superwoman as I let on to be! Needless to say, our visit went left and it hasn't been the same since. I suppose I'm selfish in that aspect! I didn't disown it. Just continued to take it one day at a time. No one could come help me in a town full of family! Or maybe, there was! I was just so used to them not doing so! I didn't even bother! So I called no one. I focused.

Two Aching Legs relying on these

10 Tremulous Fingers

To assist them to bulge.

But Ohh, No,

They INSIST ON Demanding

My Mind to Pacify Itself

To get a hold to the Disbelief.

So it could Focus On

The Here and Now

REALITY.

My Mind in Return,

Weeps Out for My Heart to do Its Part

Please Integrate Them

ALL BACK TOGETHER AGAIN.

Even then, it Can't Win.

I'm stuck, Fighting the Urge to

Fall into the Muck

I made for myself

There lies My Soul in Pieces,

Helplessly CALLING OUT for a Deposit Of Love

In Any Way, Shape, or Form.

Longing to be Refilled, Restored,

PUT BACK TOGETHER AGAIN.

My Heart is NOW VACANT

Feelings NO LONGER Occupied It

I'M NUMB.

My Mind is filled with Meaningless Memories

Of You, of Myself, of Us.

OF THIS ENTIRE SCREWED UP WORLD.

Fatigue takes OVER My Body
FROM THE INSIDE OUT.

I'm Drained.
Weary!
I am Empty.

A Hand Touches my skin,
Calming My Heart's Pace

Who is there?
I can't make out their Face.

My Legs and Fingers form into My Asana.
It was a Gentle Spirit coming into me
I RELAXED My Tense Shoulders!

The heavy shades OVER MY EYES Fall Shut
And Regain Moisture.

Under the Moonlight, I appeared
I'M NOW ALRIGHT.
The tension I felt INSIDE My Form begins to Seize.
I melt into the Dark Sky, for I know I am Light.

The Stars Twinkle in My Soul,

Slowly Making Me Whole.

Breathe In, Breathe Out.

Shake It Off, Dezy.

It's TIME TO Dance All Night!

"AND DID!"

Honey, I danced all night long to the beat of my own song! Accepting what is, letting go of what was. I maneuvered my way through a panic attack all by myself! Growth looked good on me!

Back to Texas, we flew to celebrate Christmas together as a family. That was the first time in nine months that genuine smiles were shown on their faces. We still worked through the grief process. Healed a little bit more than yesterday. But at that moment, we focused on celebrating how yesterday was now one day!

Yesterday, I was full of Energy,

Juggling 10 Obstacles at a time.

There I stood ALONE in My Fight.

No, NOT AN INCH of Help in Sight.

Or

Maybe there was

JUST NEVER REACHED OUT

Just because, I mean, didn't they see My Hands Full?

Did I wear the Garments of Strong?

So good that it FOOLED both you and me.

Didn't they see me Juggling Obstacles in the Air,

Seemingly Impossible to keep their Beat?

Wobbling on My Feet, Smiling through it All.

Just for Yesterday to NO LONGER BE

Yesterday, But Today.

Today,

I fell to My Knees as all the Obstacles Devoured Me.

I tried to PULL My Face from the Dirt,

But the Hurt, Pain, and Shame left Me Stuck

Playing the Blame Game

Calling Out ONLY My Own Name.

Today God sent me an Angel to Dig Me Out.

Lifting Bricks of Despair with its shovel of Intentionality

Dwelling in this Safe Place

I Got Too Comfortable

And Forgot to KEEP My Healing Pace

Comfortability caused me NOT to Care.

About the Who, What, When, Where, and Why.

It had me sitting still ENJOYING THE RIDE

Today, I was HELD AGAINST MY WILL.

Forced to sit my Tail Down and Heal.

Fa'real!

The buried treasures HID UNDERNEATH My Smile.

Started to Turn Loose and Fall after a while.

A new vow has come about, I'll Dance till I'm Sore

Cause God declared LOOK AT HER NOW.

There'll be NO MORE!

No More FOOLISHNESS Indeed.

I'll do the work even when it Hurts.

Because Yesterday will NO LONGER BE TODAY

Today will NO LONGER BE TODAY,

But ONE DAY.

THAT DAY COULD BE ANY DAY.

I'll be Whole and Bold!

Enough to LET GO!

Look at me, Speaking My Truth

In a Firm Tone.

Unapologetically growing into My Own.

I'll let folks in

In Real Life.

No longer WORRIED about

Who's Wrong or Who's Right?

On this day, these Triggers

WON'T REVERT ME!

Instead, I'll Walk Gracefully.

SINGING:

"YES, HONEY, WELCOME TO THE NEW ME."

The new me was on a rise! Soul work was now my life. I felt content
enough to dig up the dead bones that had turned rotten under my rug! I faced
each load of trauma with my eyes open! I kept on the whole Armor of God.
A Warrior at war, I became. Demolished all of yesterday's demons, so they
couldn't creep into my tomorrow. Peace hung around my neck as my medal
of honor! I wore it well.

I guess the boy's birth mothers could see just that through the pictures,
posts, and dances I posted on social media. An entire year later, I was
granted a full weekend with all four boys. The sounds of wrestling moves,

video game battles, mixed in with arguments, put me in an enchanted place. My fussing echoed years of fussing as I lay there tickled. We were one step closer to the family all of us secretly missed. My goal was to get that family back together one way or the other.

"I'm going to make it happen, boys," I'd say to them.

"Pinky promise."

****

Back to the schoolhouse I went to start loving on babies as I started the process of opening my home childcare back. I even planned to enroll in school again. Everything had really fallen into place. I'd sit out mesmerized in my rocking chair. I watched Pappi willingly allow the sun to grace him with its presence. Outside the house, he stayed playing basketball. I watched in awe each time Ahkhim smiled and uttered words of life.

"Did you see that, Mommy? I popped a willy, and I didn't fall," he'd say in excitement.

"There's always gonna be another mountain. I'm always gonna wanna make it move. Always gonna be an uphill battle. Sometimes I'm going to have to lose. It ain't about how fast I get there. It ain't about what's waiting on the other side. It's the climb." Miley Cyrus' song lyrics rolled off my lips. I thought about my climb, then burst into praise!

"Lord, I thank You. The word says faith without works is dead! I've been doing the work. Healing from my childhood trauma and marriage trauma. Old me trauma. Trauma on top of trauma. Thank You, Dear God, for reminding me I am worth more than rubies and diamonds! Thank You for reminding me that I am enough."

As the Sun Beamed Down its natural powers
Healing My Inner Being.

A Voice Whispered:
Aht Aht Aht
Drop it!
That DOESN'T belong to you.

Why?
BECAUSE YOU ARE ENOUGH.

Why I accepted such Burdens as Gifts
My name appeared NOWHERE ON,
Is beyond me.

Burns, Bruises, Death, and Unhealed Wounds.
Allowing him to do to us as he please
While you BEGGED on your Knees.

Wasn't Enough Fuss?

Why?
BECAUSE I AM ENOUGH

You didn't Fight with ALL YOUR MIGHT

For your God-Given Rights

That could have changed our ENTIRE LIFE.

Sigh Yes,

Times may have been hard

And although I have FINALLY let down My Guard.

That Gift You Unknowingly Gave.

Ohh, IT DOESN'T belong to me.

Why?

BECAUSE I AM ENOUGH.

I WAS ENOUGH

For you to spare each Heartbreaking Task

You took part in Against Your Family.

Your Wicked Eyes WARNED

NOT to Tell a Soul

As I Fell Off into

MY DESIGNATED HOLE.

But you see,

That Gift You Unknowingly Gave

IT DOESN'T Belong to Me.

Why?

BECAUSE I AM ENOUGH.

I WAS ENOUGH

When My Heart WANTED NOTHING

But to be Loved and Let My Love Be.

I DIDN'T DESERVE

The random Disappearing Nights,

The Toxic Fistfights.

Nor

Me Begging, Pleading, and Bargaining

For you to TREAT ME RIGHT.

No, that gift you Unknowingly Gave.

It DOESN'T Belong to Me.

Why?

BECAUSE I AM ENOUGH.

I AM ENOUGH

To Receive Love

JUST AS I DELIVERED IT.

I AM ENOUGH

To be Given Patience

As an INTENTIONAL GIFT.

Understanding as a WILLING GIFT.

Empathy as a PREPARED GIFT.

Why?

Because These Burdens Disguised as Gifts

I have Unknowingly Accepted from this World.

They DON'T Belong to Me.

Can you Guess Why?

BECAUSE I AM ENOUGH!

I had cleared out the residue from under my rug and pledged to keep it that way! I was different, lighter, I was FREE!

I will NO LONGER sweep things under the rug.

Instead, I will feel EXACTLY how I need to Feel

And swallow each Huge, Horrifying, Disgusting Pill.

I've decided to engage in this thing called

SHADOW WORK.

Apparently,

I'm to deal with MY SHIT NOW

So it doesn't Come Up Later

On My Next Ride

At the Wrong Freaking Time.

I mean.

Imagine Looking in My Eyes, telling me

You Want Me.

Yet, In Return

I'm Triggered and Questioned.

You Want Me?

Mann, Bro

All I WANT is to be FREE.

So Expect Me to be just that.

I'm going to Burst into Dance.

In the Middle of Nowhere.

As you Smile in AWE

Staring Right There.

Expect Me to Cry in Your Presence

When life gets to be Too Much.

Because between the Two of Us,

We shouldn't have to Be Tough.

We can just BE FREE.

Expect Me to be Mad on ANY Given Day

Because we're Allowed to be

When life DOESN'T go our way.

Of course, I'll get Past It

Every Single Time and Smile

I will ALWAYS find Peace

AFTER A WHILE.

Let's love and be loved on without limits, keeping in mind that time has no modifications.

So Let's Get With It! Let's be Self-Driven!

LET'S BE FREE.

Call me a Hippie if you please,

But in the end, WE SHOULD AGREE

There is NO SUCH BOX we're Planted In.

I'm DONE REQUESTING Let Me Be.

Baby, don't you know I'm a Butterfly?

I've shredded those skins, Way Back When!

We're talking about NOW,

NOT THEN.

Try learning from nature in every which way. Don't you hear the wind howling, demanding you to "Just Be Free."

Dance in the Rain and LET GO of the Pain

So you can "JUST BE FREE."

Bask in the Sun for Fun

Affirm to yourself.

I am NO LONGER bound

My time IS NOW.

I am as FREE as a Butterfly!

On My Worst and Best Days.

Whether you Agree or Not

Is FINE with Me

Just know that, Miss Rita.

IS FINALLY FREE.

I was on a roll, I was as free as a bird. Till I no longer wanted to be! I wanted to be loved on again! Touched in places I forgot sent chills up my spine! I wanted what I wanted, so I went out to find it!

I went and captured the Old Virgin Islands. He was a man's man! Handsome Fella. Well established, ready to fall in love!

Hell, who was I kidding? I wanted what I wanted, when I wanted it! Unfortunately, he didn't turn my switch back on. So, Old Virgin Island came and went!

Can you believe
I thought your Hands were Big Enough
To hold the Shattered Pieces
GRIEF LEFT My Heart In.

That's the Strength you've seen in me
FORCEFULLY WEAR
Would be Swapped Out for SOFTNESS at its Best.

Then I could finally rest as you led all the pieces back into the pretty picture it once painted.

- But now tainted-

Tahh…

Turns out your pieces were weighing you down, and you were

expecting me to turn your smile upside down.

On a PEDAL STOOL you have Placed Me,

Ignoring the Flaws that Dresses Me,

Declaring to the World

There ISN'T A THING WRONG with Me.

The Smile.

The smile you wear seems as if I've gifted it to you wrapped in the prettiest wrapper.

Designed to make your Heartbeat.

(Sigh)

I suppose maybe it's why you CAN'T ACTUALLY

See Me.

Here I STAND before you,

The NEW CURE to your Deadly Disease

The RUNETH OVER from your Cup.

I have made your World OK.

Any CHAOS has been Driven Away,

Flooded with PEACE All Day, Every Day.

Making My Superwoman Cape fit me.

There I LAY IN Agony,

Silently Begging for someone to come

AND SIMPLY SEE ME.

PLEASE.

Stop making me your EVERYTHING.

When you CAN'T even be My Little Bit.

Don't PLACE your Heart in my hands

Expecting Constant Wins,

Then Grow to DESPISE ME

When I've DROPPED ALL I'VE HELD.

I SINCERELY APOLOGIZE.

But Oh Well.

Look at me.

I'm NOT Perfect,

No Matter how much Honey Drizzles from My Lips

When I Speak.

I swear, I make just as many mistakes as you. Honey! No one is better than you. Don't you know you walk in the same grace and mercy as we all do?

Yes,

I Love, Just Love,

But I Love You for you.

So look at Me Bro-

And Love Me Too-

Look!

Maybe that's something you.

Just DON'T have the Capacity for.

It's Cool Boo

You know what I Stand On.

One Monkey...

DON'T STOP NO SHOW.

So do us Both a Favor

Walk ON OUT that Door.

Because if you CAN'T

Love and See Me!

FOR ME.

It's Cool.

I WON'T Be Moved

I'll just continue to Make It Do

WHAT I ALWAYS DO!

Oh, but hard heads definitely make some soft tails! I tried dating again. Even considered letting the past back in! Till I got my stuff together and had to remember when!

Conversations that you be like.

No, DON'T You Remember?

Remember,

When you FLEW IN as My Shining Knight

Snatched My Knife

As I SO CLOSELY Took My Own Life.

Demanded Me to get it Right.

I was nearly 6 feet under, wearing a painted smile, chilling in the midst of my Thunder.

I bet you wondered.

Is this Real or Make Believe?

No, Darling, your eyes DIDN'T DECEIVE.

You must remember how I was a complicated melody playing your favorite song.

Remember,

How you Played your Part

Grabbing at My Heart,

Forcing Me to Sing Along?

I was it for you Once Before

Then I Remembered

You got your Thrill,

So gone were All Your Feels.

I remember, don't you?

I remember the Ride of a Lifetime,

Where I ACTED as if you were Mine.

You know WAY MORE than a Friend.

Yet, in the back of my mind

I knew it would SOON END.

After all, You were Playing Pretend.

And the Truth:

Me.

OH, I WAS JUST YOUR FRIEND.

Don't you remember?

Remember the SUMMARY of Our Time Spent

Or did it QUICKLY become the past

And the MEMORIES that Came and Went?

Of course, I REMEMBER IT ALL

So Pure and Clear.

I wanted you Near

That part you MOST DIDN'T HEAR.

Don't you remember how fast you Grew

TO DESPISE ME?

No GRACE given

As we both kept on Sinning.

Shit!

I remember how I DIDN'T take that Lightly.

Because REGARDLESS of my flaws,

My Love is a Work of Art.

There is NO ONE LIKE ME.

You Better Remember THAT, Honey?

REMEMBER THAT!

I sure as hell remembered. It was embedded in me. I refuse to accept
what was waiting for me after 10 years and a hiccup of commitment. No

longer did I yearn to be refilled, restored, put back together again. Receiving an ounce back in reciprocation was now a bare minimum that couldn't be met.

"What kind of dating pool was I fishing out of?" I'd ask myself.

I went about it the wrong way. I desired to have someone again! Then I heard a song. My heart's song.

Night fell upon Me

And there "YOU" were

HOLDING Me So Closely.

I felt my body beginning to DISSOLVE

As I listened to the Symphonies of My Heart's Song.

"Just Come to Me Where You Belong."

It played a tune, Full of Rejection.

Making me wonder,

Did I miss My BLESSING?

The If, Ands, But's, and Whats.

Started to develop a Loud Constant Pattern.

I Quenched with ANXIETY each time

A KNOT developed in the Pit of My Belly.

Like frequent times, LIFE LEFT ME LONELY.

"You" are a TASTE I've started to feen

Yet, I don't even know what

What I'm LONGING to Taste.

A Piece to My Puzzle

I DIDN'T KNOW EXISTED.

My Heart's Song STOPPED playing along.

"Just Come to Me, Where You Belong."

My Body and Soul JOINED in Unison,

Making My Head Spin.

My body LAY STILL under the stars.

If only my love COULD SOON be ours.

I sang out, Hoping My Heart

Would Follow.

"Come to Me Where You Belong."

It didn't. My words BEGIN to FADE.

I decided NOT to activate the Grenade.

Leaving the Past in the Past,

Remembering to Stop Rushing into the "Idea of Love"

TOO FAST.

So I'll Make A WISH

Upon the Stars.

And pray "YOU" catch it wherever you are.

Whether NEAR or FAR.

For My NEW Heart's Song.

"Basking in God's Love is Where You Belong."

It WON'T Scar.

My Mind, Body, Heart, and Soul.

Now Seemed to be WHOLE.

"Basking in God's love is where you belong."

A Song of Love, Joy, and Peace.

Because that's what My NEW Heart Song.

"Basking in God's Love is Where You Belong."

Has Delivered Again to Me.

God reminded me that with Him is where I belong. Commanded I stop searching and continue to heal. I got somewhere and sat down so I could be still.

It's why when Big Country's Day came around, I didn't go partake in serving. I sat right there at the Church House, absorbing the message. Palms 147: 3 "God heals the broken-hearted and binds up their wounds."

But every time the Lord begins to heal you, you go picking at the wound, dwelling on the past.

Stage One of the wound healing cycle is Hemostasis: Stop the bleeding to prevent further harm to the wound.

Stage Two: Inflammation. Damaged cells release chemicals that attract immune cells to remove debris, bacteria, and damaged tissues, resulting in swelling, redness, and pain.

Stage 3: Proliferation. New tissues are built to fill the wounds. Skin cells grow over the new tissues, eventually closing the wound.

Stage 4: Remodeling. The final phase focuses on strengthening and remodeling the new tissues.

"Which one are you at?" the pastor called out.

I had just started phase three. Going to be a willing vessel for the heavy energy to be transferred to me was a no-no. That meant I'd have had to expose my wound and start my healing journey again.

Isaiah 43:18-19 (NIV) "Forget the former things, do not dwell on the past. See, I am doing a new thing! Now it springs up; do you not perceive it? I am making a way in the wilderness and streams in the wasteland."

I soaked in the entire message with an Amen, wiping my tears, and confirmed my decision of absence.

****

Six months into the new year, Happy 34th Birthday to me. My gift happened to be a platonic friendship from the schoolhouse. We helped each other heal in the presence of God. I traded my loneliness for late nights out on the town and early mornings at the church house, being fed the Word. I stood on, it's not what you do, it's how you do it!

She connected the boys and me to a wonderful family counselor who helped us tremendously. Therapy taught me how valuable my voice was, so I started to use it.

Guess What, Y'all?
I have FOUND My Voice.

Can you believe it was Buried
Under People Pleasing, Lack of Boundaries,
And Conflict Avoidance?

Yeah, you see, when I FINALLY FOUND IT,
I had to Fight it with ALL My Might,
Cuz this Doggone Voice of Mine
JUST WOULDN'T DO RIGHT.

Scared it would banish the Fake Connection
I Made Real.

You know,
The Same Connection
That once made Me Feel
SAFE ENOUGH TO HEAL.

It Whispered.

Something is Better than Nothing.

So let's JUST KEEP ON Trucking,

Fronting till they see Your Worth.

No Biggie,

You're Strong,

IT WON'T EVEN HURT.

No, No, No, Speak Up Voice

You See.

You MUST help me

Show these Lil Uglies

They CAN NO LONGER HALF

Love Me.

Contacting me just because they WANT SOMETHING.

Making Me SMILE just enough to

Forget About the Pain.

But later

Got me remembering how much

My Love is All In Vain.

But it's cool

Cuz I have FOUND My Voice, Y'all!

I pulled it by his Timid Horns

Making it Express Itself

SOMEHOW, SOMEWAY.

Paragraphs TURNED into Books.

That they didn't even Give One Look.

Silent Cries under the Moonlight Sky

Became the Usual.

So, I went and I pulled a Bit More

Then Boom!

Hell, I FELL to the Floor!

I guess I pulled that joker out a Little Too Fast.

Because it has respectfully told everyone.

TO KISS MY ASS!

Man, I have FOUND My Voice, Y'all.

It screamed NO, it's Too Late.

Don't come up in My Face.

'Cause Baby, I've Caught On

So you can NO LONGER Manipulate.

Play the Victim as you please.

I applaud each Punch, Kick, and Rock.

My Voice has been THROWN in Self-Defense.

She's out now, Standing Boldly,

And WILL NOT MISS!

The Lord may have said,

Turn the Other Cheek.

But Honey,

I have FOUND My Voice.

So Baby, I remembered how Worthy

God has Deemed Me.

You can bet I'll be

Holding on to My Voice Tight.

Standing on the fact that

I can COURAGEOUSLY SPEAK to the Darkness

YET STILL BE LIGHT!

Honey, I started talking, and that was all she wrote! I was done being taken advantage of. I no longer settle for less. I expected what I deserved. The very best.

My cousin moved to Texas for a fresh start, and I became a bit sassier. The backlash had me going back to backtrack and apologize for speaking my mind.

Kewanis would say, "Dezy, fuck them, you are not sorry."

He was right, I wasn't. Moving forward, I only spoke what I meant and meant what I said. Forced empathy was worse than no empathy.

The Lord sent him to me! The weight of backlash from speaking up got heavy! He caught me when old habits refused to die hard, and bed rotting became addictive again! Laughter was the medicine he issued that I'd take a sip of instead of my pity!

I prayed heavily for my boys' healing because, although I saw fast-paced healing in myself, I couldn't in them. Pappi worked on obtaining a spot on the basketball team. He was still on antidepressants. He needed assistance managing that new school and a fresh start all over again. Ahkhim started to fall in love with basketball during the day, then grief disturbed his dreams at night. His Daddy's star became his favorite visiting spot. The sorrow met him there, pulling me in to join in on one accord. Aiden and Jaylon were two hours away. Whenever my energy spiked, I'd go get them on weekends. I enjoyed the hellos, but the goodbyes were difficult. The boys wanted to stay. I wanted them to stay. Ahkhim needed him to stay! They missed being together. But I wasn't driving the bus anymore. God was. So, I did as I could when I had them. I'd remind them who their father and I raised them to be when they fall astray. I kept bringing them back to what they knew. God!

It's amazing how my smile continued to pollute this World's lowest vibration. Uplifting all that got a drift of it. I made this shit look easy. Hell, if only they knew how I'd lie down and listen to the sounds of the boy's sound effects travel through the house. Reflecting! It seemed to hit me like a ton of bricks all over again! I needed Lavarius, and although I don't believe in ghosts! There he was!

I DON'T BELIEVE in Ghosts.

But last night, One Walked through my door

And SAT on my bed.

You wouldn't BELIEVE the things he said.

Tahh! Or Was it Me?

Because after I Laid Eyes On that Joker.

I got to Fussing and Fighting, you see.

Screaming,

How dare you LEAVE that oldest boy

To figure out this Terrifying Transition to Manhood!

Didn't you HEAR his silent songs?

Of Should A-- Would A-- Could Haves?

He was PUSHED to Grow Up and take your place.

Weighed down by the Hands of Grief,

Frightened by its Face.

He ran to death with a Bargaining Soul.

Desiring to be Awarded to you

To make this Family WHOLE.

But just like you, today,

Death had NOTHING to Say.

Echoes of Darkness FILLED the Room.

Chills sent me INTO Discombobulation.

As I sat Questioning,

Do I really see what I see?

Because I DON'T BELIEVE in Ghosts.

But there stood that Country Joker in his Superman Cape.

Asking me if I'm Okay

Tahh! You have got to be kidding me.

You mean you don't see the Trauma that Red Boy Holds?

How he CAN'T seem to Shake It.

Confused about Stability, settling for his Old Reality.

Pants Sagging, False Flagging.

Yet, here I stand with Quivering Limbs,

DOING THE VERY BEST I CAN.

Wondering when the Flow of Residue

From Losing you

WILL END?

Fighting hard for him to be FREE.

Reminding him of who we raised

HIM TO BE

But all we need you to do is to STOP this Hoax.

Come Home. It's been 2 Years TOO LONG.

Because like I said,

I DON'T BELIEVE IN GHOSTS.

How can I when I see you Every Day?

That Chocolate Twin of yours puts on our blues

As we DANCED the Night Away.

Do you know some nights?

He wakes up Sweaty and Frantic?

Hearing Emone-Emone-Emone

Like a BROKEN RECORD.

It's funny how his mouth can't say it

Because SOMEWAY, SOMEHOW,

I've Imprinted Myself on him.

His caring Stocky Statue hides it all.

The Tears of Grief, Stuck in Disbelief

That he PURPOSEFULLY Holds Back,

Won't ALLOW him to Mourn you.

So what the HELL Am I Supposed to Do?

Continue to Hold Them in My Arms

As we Cry to the Rhythm of

OUR BROKEN HEARTS?

Four boys Linked to Despair. I Mean Grief.

I mean a life WITHOUT their Dad,

With ONLY a Mama.

A Mama who holds her Breath,

Longing to Breathe.

Who's so over Grief?

Yet MUST CONTINUE to Smile and Bear

When ALL she wants is AIR!

NO! I DON'T BELIEVE IN GHOSTS.

But a Fine Ass Man,

Black as night held me with Reassurance,

Kissed Me with Everything Gonna Be Alright.

Just Keep On Keeping On.

Don't lose the Faith in your Sight.

Tahh! Push through MY ASS!

Have you seen your Fat Baby these days?

Notice how his Smile is Fabricated

How being social is Entirely Overrated.

Our Baby Boy is tired of swimming in his Pool of Sorrows

Baptizing the fragment of his happiness

Into a Sea of Bittersweet Memories

JUST TO BE CLOSE TO YOU.

His COMFORT LIES

When he's Resting His Eyes

In Dreamland.

There, he's Daddy's Baby Again.

NO, I DON'T BELIEVE IN GHOSTS

But on my Hands and Knees,

I PLEADED to My Superman.

I can only do so much.

Yet STILL Show Face.

I need you HERE to help me WIN THIS RACE.

Shit! I Dance, Dogging Burdens
Meant to make Me Stuck.

But just like the Moon needs the Sun
For Illumination.
Please come help raise My Vibration.

Place that weighted Blanket of Skin On Mine.
Freeze Time.
COME BACK to be Mine Again.
ONE LAST TIME!

NOPE. HELL NO, I DON'T BELIEVE IN GHOSTS.
But that Confident Husband of mine
Came Jigging through the door

As the boys jumped his Out-Of-Shape Tail
Again and Again.

The Love of My Life,
Who made Me His Wife
Handed me a Drink with a Wink
I Watched with Glee.

Not At All!
WE DON'T BELIEVE IN GHOSTS.

But there we stood.

As the Whispers of Our Hearts

Uttered their FINAL Goodbyes

His presence may have Faded Away,

But so was Our Dismay

It was REPLACED with Peace.

Free from our Unwavering Faith

In God We Trust ALWAYS WILL,

Down in the Valley

Or On Top of the Hills.

NO, WE DON'T BELIEVE IN GHOSTS.

But My Superman SWOOPED RIGHT IN,

Just in time for US ALL TO SAY.

Daddy--Husband--Pette--Big County

Lavarius

Happy Father's Day!

Continue to Soar High

And Let Your Light Shine!

PART FOUR

Just Out Here Living!

"Gone are the chains that were holding me. Gone is the person I used to be! Freed from all fears by God's perfect love. THIS IS MY EXODUS! THIS IS MY EXODUS!"

-Israel Hartong!-

Once I got out of God's way, situations caused the state to grant me my family back! Growing around grief! Next mission!

It marked Lavarius's and my 12th wedding anniversary! Each year, we took family pictures to mark the day our family became one. Although we lost this tradition when our family began to fall apart. We decided in therapy as a family that we'd bring it back. We discussed color schemes and themes. Car club colors and vest became the top choice. We decided, although Lavarius was gone! He would still be included in our family pictures.

There were two car club vests. One was given to the mother and the other to the father. We borrowed the vest the father had. That vest just so happened to be the vest. I pulled out of his truck. Patches missing. Burnt pieces stained. The smell of sulfur covered it. "I thought they fixed it!" I exclaimed, fading back into the very moment I pulled it out. We all released with tears of whatever emotions wanted to be freed at that time. No longer did I hide the life falling down my face. I needed them to know. We were all in this together.

We smiled for the camera. Cried for the camera and frowned for the camera. Happy Anniversary. Happy New Year's Eve. Happy 2025. We were off to new beginnings.

My home childcare had taken off, back loving on the babies in my home, my way. There were only two ladies in town I fooled with. Ms. Cynthia and Dominique. They helped put the word out, and I was now a credible prospect to take care of their children. They were my support system who saw a need and filled it! Confirmation kissed my forehead with genuine words, and I spoke to them. "Thank you, ladies, I have finally found my tribe!"

A year later, we graduated from family therapy. The boys were taught techniques on how to properly use their outlets. Health and Wellness activities when grief is trying to overrun them. They were turning into the vibrant boys I once knew them to be. I had to tell the world, look out, my boys were coming.

Dear World.

If I WANTED Your Opinion.

I'd ASK for it.

The way I raised my Young Man.

May be SOFT to you.

But Ohh,

Dear World of Ours.

You are HARD ENOUGH.

So, I'll CONTINUE to

Hand out Hugs and Kisses.

Disciplined them with My Rod of Love

When they DON'T LISTEN.

Reassuring them in Every Which Way.

Not putting them down.

EVERY SINGLE DAY.

Dear World.

The mark you have placed

On their Melanin Skin.

Have been Removed by the Hands

Of A Praying Mother

From the Top of their Heads

To the Soles of their Feet

For they have been

Fearfully and Wonderfully Made.

Blessed and Highly Favored

Trained up in a way,

Which they Shall NOT Depart.

Dear World of Ours!

You can't have their Courageous Ways,

Nor their Bold Voices of Integrity.

You DON'T have their Permission to Poison

Their minds with Deceitful Lies,

SO PLEASE STOP WASTING YOUR TIME.

Dear World.

Despite what you think about Black Boys.

My boys are Book Smart, Street Smart,

They Own Right from Wrong Smarts.

Discernment is in their Walk.

Humbleness in their Talk.

Go On and Catch a Glimpse

Of that Twinkle in their Eyes

As you Walk On By.

PLEASE Step to the Side!

But Remember Now, World.

If they WANTED, Your Opinion

Guess What?

THEY'D ASK FOR IT!

Just like that, the boys were soaring. Ahkhim danced with Jaylon. Did his wrestling moves on each other. Made buzzer sounds shots in basketball. So confident. Jaylon cooked our favorite meals. Happy to assist with fixing anything around the house! Adein played all the latest blues and educated us on all kinds of helicopters and cars. Speech improved; he no longer held back his emotions. He found himself a new grove. Pappi had a little girlfriend, played basketball while passing all his AP/dual credit classes!

The Lord told me a long time ago! Seek first the Kingdom of Heaven, and all would line up! I saw the proof in the pudding. It was in the boys' growth, in their smiles, in each twinkle in their eyes. I was immersed in gratitude.

"Thank You, God! Anything You want me to do, I'll do it, Lord. Anything You don't want me to do. Just say the word and it's over with. I want to live for You, Oh God! Your will over my life is what I long to bask in. You have been so good to me, Lord! Clean me up to Your liking. Burn all that once was, so there will be room for what's to come." I ended with a Thank You as the lyrics of an Amen came pouring out of my mouth.

"I want to be tried by fire to purify. Please take whatever You desire, Lord, here is my life."

I sat out by a fire with my family as we celebrated all that was ours, is ours, and all that is to come. This is only the beginning.

****

Pappi: "Ma, where you going looking like that"?

"I swear my Daddy was all the way in Green Bay," I laughed.

"I'm just saying, you haven't been out in a while now, all of a sudden you're out here taking pictures and stuff," he said.

"I am just going to meet a friend, please get out of my business," I smirked.

"I'm glad, I have your location," he said, walking away.

I couldn't help but laugh at him. It was nice to be cared for, but annoying at the same time. *Who did he think he was? He was my firstborn, not the other way around, but I let him have it as I always did. After all, he was my Pappi!"*

He wasn't telling a story. I hadn't been out in a while. The dating pool had scared me away; it made me give up on love. I gave just to be sucked dry. The more I went out, the more I felt deep in my soul that love wasn't for me. My switch just wouldn't turn back on. I had a wall up that wasn't falling anytime soon. But, I suppose I had to start somewhere, regardless of my crooked heart.

The Summer Breeze

My Crooked Heart once blew

Seems as if it's turned into the Thickest Ice Wall,

Refusing to Fall.

No longer do I have the Desire

To Love On You.

To be the Supplier of our needs.

To speak to You EVER So Gently.

Putting Your Mind at Ease.

The Voided Oath, I once gave…

Now Gone

To only add Joy and Peace into your life.

That Any Time.

Any time I TOOK AWAY from such.

Well, that just meant

MY TIME WAS UP.

But now, here I Present Myself to you.

No reflexes to the Actions of Love thrown at me.

No Sight to See

When someone is Genuinely showing that

THEY CARE FOR ME.

You see, Bro!

I've Loved, I've Loved, I've Loved,

AND I'VE LOVED SOME MORE.

Now that Cold Day in Hell

Has APPEARED Out of Nowhere.

Making me utter one "Oh, Well" in Self-Defense

As I sit, SO CONFUSED about the Way I Feel.

Like Man.

THIS SHIT JUST CAN'T BE REAL!

My Old Ways.

My Old Ways have PASSED AWAY.

Recreated as this THICK Ice Wall

That has made Me New.

I Swear.

I Swear, behind it Lie Bittersweet

Pieces of Gold.

I gave TOO FREELY to this World.

A NAÏVE FOOL Indeed.

That is What I Have Been Told.

But Now.

But now, SOMEHOW, SOMEWAY.

I'm Protecting It All.

As I Reap the Fruits of My Own Hard Labor.

Still Dreading the Delightful Day.

When someone Comes and Pricks

This Thick Ice Wall Away.

I Swear.

I swear it SCARES Me so badly.

Because I know I should Love

AND NOT RUN.

But I WELCOME FEAR with open arms,

Because I'm Safe, ALTHOUGH I'm Bound.

I just feel like,

NO RECIPROCATION.

Of ANY Love Lies within Me.

I've given ALL I COULD to this World.

But I Was Used Up.

Now my switch is TURNED OFF.

I'm DEPLETED, on E.

Feeling like NO. HELL NO!

No One or Nothing

Can't get SHIT ELSE from Me.

Don't Worry, the EXIT OUT of my life

You will NEVER have to find.

It's why I Humbly Expressed this ALL TO YOU NOW

SO YOU WON'T WASTE YOUR TIME.

One day,

This Thick Ice Wall

WILL FINALLY DISSOLVE.

One day,

I'll LOVE AGAIN

And ALLOW Love to Love Me.

Until then.

This is a WARNING.

From a good girl Turned Numb.

SAVE YOURSELF.

AND RUN.

Because Yes, Honey.

I Admit It.

I AM THROUGH WITH LOVE.

I made this clear in our intriguing conversation before I left the coffee shop! I suppose we both came to a mutual agreement. Friends with benefits sounded great. Kenni came in dressed in a type of elegance I hadn't seen before!

"Pardon my tardiness." Blessed my ears as this yellow piece of beauty sat across from me.

The orange and yellow complemented the smile, talking to me, which made it easy for minutes to turn into hours. The booth was at our mercy; in it, a connection was made that compelled me to fully insert myself into this equation.

"Just have fun, Dez," I reminded myself.

That's the only expectation I held on to. Nothing else was asked of me till Kenni asked me to move in closer and take a deep breath. I complied as the nape of my neck became surrounded with five reasons why I was right where I needed to be! The coffee shop was dense, lights low, music playing beneath our gentle voices. In the booth, we continued playing out one of my favorite fantasies. Jumping out of myself, watching in satisfaction. I was proud of the flow I maintained. Staying present, enjoying the moment.

On to the park we escaped, not wanting the day to end. More walks and talks mixed in with butterflies I hadn't felt in years. After numerous dates and failed establishments, before they even began. I initiated my captivity right under the sun's kisses. You could say it was something like a ménage à trois lost in its rays, being healed with its light. Just having fun, right? Or was I so drawn in by the floating minerals of floating ecstasy of our connection that it really had me questioning. Was I through with love?

"Love don't live here anymore.

Just the vacancy.

No, love doesn't live here anymore."

-Faith Evans-

Hmm, I don't know about that.

See, love has ALWAYS lived here.

FROZEN,

But with the Heat from the Flames

The actions of Love Ignited it can be Thawed

Yes. Mmm-Hmm.

It may have been Buried Under FLAWS I created

And Imperfections assigned to me

But with the Hands of Acceptance

Willing to Put in the Work,

It Can Be Found.

"LOVE DOESN'T LIVE HERE ANYMORE."

Tahh! Ohh No. That is a Lie!

Society made me believe such.

After Love Bruised, Beat, and 'Bout Broke Me Down.

But No, Ma'am

I CAN'T ALLOW this World Full of Impostors

Presenting themselves in front of Balloon Poppers.

For Validations, Convince Me OTHERWISE.

LOVE LIVES HERE, BOO!

Hmm...

You think it's INSANE to say

Keep bringing me Flowers just to see My Smile.

Nawwww

Dezy, You Can't Say That!

SHIT!

Will Kenni or Whoever Else

Be Wasting their Time?

Only Receiving Gratitude,

Wondering if your Heart

Will EVER Bust a Move, Dezy?

(Sigh)

Thinking of such is

ALREADY TOO MUCH

On My Plate.

Because now,

I just CAN'T GO at such a Fast Rate.

Or maybe it's just that I Won't Rush Fate.

And who the Hell are we

To ask ANYONE to wait, Dezy?

MAYBE LOVE DOESN'T LIVE HERE ANYMORE!

I suppose LOVE AND I had an Understanding.

If It Didn't Bother Me,

I sure as Hell wasn't going to

BOTHER IT!

****

The stone had finally been placed down on Lavarius's resting spot. I held firm to my belief. I didn't feel the need to go and see it, not even once. I didn't feel the need to visit his spot, not even once. But I know it held the closure the boys needed. Ahkhim verified it with a letter to his daddy that he requested to read to him. Their wishes were really my command.

Back in Arkansas, we were! Checking right into the hotel, the reminder of our last visit hit me. I stared at the bed, feeling the heaviness falling over me. Tempted to dive into my sea of surrendering. Instead, I tapped into my faith and pushed away the fear! "By God's stripes, you have been healed." I heard my Granny's voice. If she did nothing else, she taught me how to be a faithful steward of God's army. There was no time to waste. The predicted rainfall wouldn't force this trip to be in vain. When we arrived at the commentary. The boys didn't wait for my cue to hop out of the car. They were anxious to quiet the void that yelled at them in spurts when it received no attention. It wasn't hard to locate him; his sight had been decked out with beautiful lights and flowers. Shining while dust settled on the other headstones. Even in his death, Ms. Leeann didn't play that.

The boys: silenced. Staring, speaking words only meant for their father's ears. No tears were shed. Lots of kisses were blown, pictures had been taken, and hugs given. I sat in anticipation. Were their floodgates going to burst? Was I going to have to swoop in and catch them before they fell? Were words of anger going to come crushing down their lips, cursing me in rounds of frustration, one by one, for the very imagery they stood in silence gazing at?

But no, nothing. A gust of wind blew, sending warm chills over us. His solar lights lit, then went off. We turned around, looking at each other wearing expressions of awe. No one smiled but me. Despite their hidden emotions, they knew it was him. Their walk back to the car was a bit lighter. Maybe I didn't believe in such a thing. But it sure uplifted me. Closer to closure than I ever thought I could be. Watching the boys depart without words, I took a deep breath in and out like a snake. The Superman symbol that matched my ankle stood out so nobly on his headstone. It was time I sang to him a brand-new song.

"Goodbye, Lavarius, and all that I held onto in you. Numerous unidentified emotions still clog my posture as I position myself upright! One thing I know for certain is that you loved me, and I loved you! You'll always be engraved in my heart. But I can't let you fill it anymore. I've used it as a crutch. Limping on your love as if you'll reappear and fulfill all my desires as you once did. That we'd be in love all over again! Family united! Vacationing in Mexico on the beach as a redo. This time, I'd allow you to hold my hand while watching the boys build sandcastles. I promise I won't fuss about it being so sweaty. Just enjoying each other again, while you show favoritism to that fat baby. (Sigh) Unfortunately, reality has come to check me. Demanding I plant my feet and ground myself in it. I realize it's time for me to say my goodbyes. Move on and truly live my life! I love you, Superman, you know I do. I was your Wife. Maybe I'll be that again for you, but better, in another life. Please forgive me if it hurts. But the show I made you the lead in. Oh, my Superman, that show must end!"

Like the floating fragments of acid in my belly trying to escape through my esophagus. Like the buildup of gas rising into my chest, inducing symptoms of cardiac arrest. There beat these words behind my forcefully closed doors, unable to be released.

"Goodbye. Goodbye. Goodbye."

I sat Politely Positioned for you to initiate such.

Inflicting CONSTANT PAIN

On My Heart.

Comfortably sitting in the Rain, fueled by Fear

Kept me from Doing My Part.

The years I spent Holding You Hostage

Attracted my DISPLACED TRAUMA.

Stashed Away to Heal

On Another Day.

Free At Last, you are.

Like the caged bird that Once Sang.

GOODBYE. GOODBYE. GOODBYE.

GOODBYE

Now felt as Important

As each Pen Stroke, I Wrote.

As peaceful as the Jazzy Sounds,

The Saxophone Rewarded My Ears

WITH GOOD VIBES ONLY.

GOODBYE. GOODBYE. GOODBYE.

Goodbye made My Soul Whole

Kissed Me All Over,

Thanking My Entire Being

FOR BEING BOLD.

GOODBYE, SUPERMAN.

GOODBYE. GOODBYE. GOODBYE.

Freeing up that space in my heart made more room for me to fall in love with myself, catching a glimpse in the mirror every morning gave me confidence like no other. Affirmations began to roll off my tongue, saturating my soul with easy energy. Life was starting to be worth living again. I uplifted my body in indescribable ways for doing so.

Dear Eyes,

I adore each TWINKLE you give off.

Making themselves known

IN THE DARKEST SKIES.

Do you see how others

Get caught in your Beauty?

Lost in the Gaze,

Chanting Starlight, Star Bright,

You're the MOST Dazzling Star

I've Seen ALL Night.

I Wish I May

I Wish I Might

Have this Wish I've Wished Tonight.

Ohh Lips.

The Pink Juicy Fullness

Forms the Softness of the Most Delectable Kisses.

SWEET LIKE HONEYDEW

The Hips and Thighs

That shape My Outer Being

Are Perfectly Poetically Placed

In its Rightful Positions.

NOTHING MORE,

NOTHING LESS.

To my mind, I say: Stay Inquisitive

ALL DAY, EVERY DAY

Remember ALL of the Life Lessons

As well as the Victories You've Won

In the valley, while being Tested.

Ol Limbs of Mine.

May you swing your arms

To the Rhythm of your Leg's Confidence.

Walking Proudly, Up Tall!

Chin up. Regardless of whether you Fall!

Being Unapologetically You

In the world that Shames You

For just that, Boo.

Ohh 2 My Soul: Continue to be Bold.

I admire your DETERMINATION to be
Young, Wild, and Free,
Just out here, Living
Traveling Life's Mysterious Journey.

Look at you!
Allowing this New Heart Transplant to do its part
Constantly Pumping Flows of Love,
Even when it's Hard.

Dear Me:
From the Crown of your Head
To the Soles of your Feet.

You are Rare Boo.
It's ALL BECAUSE you Love like you do.

So Girl Boo!
Whoever can't get Jiggy With It.

Hell,
Chuck up the Deuces
AND WISH THEM WELL.

I became so whole within myself. No one else was needed! Not even wanted. I was okay with going out to see what I could do. Not necessarily doing what I can do. You know, just a friend to kick it with. Nothing beneath the surface of dinner and a movie. Netflix and chilling.

Well, then Kenni's love became relentless! Anticipating my needs was the new normal. Being seen for who I was beneath the smile I wore was sincerely a dream come true. I was accepted with open arms, inviting me to stay awhile. To relax and put my feet up. This was the moment I had been waiting for.

I always thought acts of service were the way to my heart. Help me accomplish all the piles stacked on my plate. Allow me to sit down and take a break. Turns out, it was me retiring my superwoman cape. I was gifted someone who reassured me that I didn't have to do it all by myself. Unfamiliar, yet fulfilling. What was this feeling? Lust? Like? Or was it really love? I wasn't sure. At this point, I didn't pay any attention to it. I was mesmerized by the eyes looking back at me. I accepted the invitation, then gave one in return!

"Won't you stay a while?" I offered.

You're like my favorite Caramel Cream Chew,
The way I study you, Through and Through.

You softly sang,
Sweet Reassurance in My Ear.
Your Gleeful Aroma is Drawing Me Near.

Your Watchful Eyes are on alert.

While your Attentive Ears

Listen to My Heart's Cue

Your Arms Wrap Me Up

In Love and Light

Replacing ALL Negative Energy

In My Body.

Sheesh.

This Feels So Right.

The way you enhance My Smile,

I fearfully invite you Into My Life.

Please Stay Awhile.

Let's Exchange Energies

While We Ride

THE SAME FREQUENCY.

No need to give it a Name

Was Understood,

NEED NOT BE EXPLAINED.

I'll Give Myself to You.

You Give Yourself to Me.

We'll let things Flow.

As we BOTH separately grow

Remembering whatever is Meant to Be

WILL SIMPLY BE!

That is the way I left it. I was no longer going to overthink this! I did it numerous times. Wishing my Granny were here, so I could dial up her line. But her spirit lay in mine, so I knew exactly what to do.

My random Overthinking be like:

Is it TOO SOON for me to Let Go?

Closing One Door to Open Another.

Of course, I CAN'T replace him.

It's just Ahhhhh!

If ONLY My Granny were here to

Tell Me What to Do.

To lighten this Load of Guilt

And Demand Me

"Girl, Get A Dog-On Grip."

There I Go, Spiraling Again,

Conjuring up All the way to Sabotage My Entire Life

ALL OVER AGAIN.

My mind is caught in the Middle of a Stampede,

Trying to Dodge the Feet

Of my own Intrusive Thoughts.

What if it's really OUR TIME to Shine,

Our Season of Love, Our Right Place

AT THE RIGHT TIME?

Or

Could Love REALLY BE this Blind?

Throwing Lessons at My Heart,

Yelling Abort! Abort!

Showing warning BEFORE Destruction.

Or is it Just My Mind that keeps being

A Damn Disruption?

My random Overthinking be like:

Would Granny tell me,

"Girl, Hush, Slow Down.

You're in TOO MUCH of a Rush."

Or would she utter, "Go Flutter, Beautiful Queen,

Spread your Wings and Be Free."

"Welcome being Loved On as you so
Deservingly Desire to be."
Ohh, these Thoughts are REALLY
Starting to Get to Me!

Under the Sun I Lay STILL
As ALL the Thoughts
Fighting for my Undivided Attention
FINALLY, HALTS.

There Will ALWAYS Be
A Battle Between the Two of Us.

It's just what it is.
My Overthinking be like:
Hmm, I think Granny would say.

"Go with the Flow and Follow your Heart.
Inside there Lies Your Savior
WHO WILL NEVER DEPART."

So, I take Heed to the Thought of her Words
And Let Go of my random OVERTHINKING
That's CLEARLY for the Birds.

Who the Son SETS FREE is Free Indeed.

So, I'll ALLOW My Mind to Run Wild

Till it's Tired

While I Focus On My Heartbeat.

I'll pledge to Live Life

WITHOUT REGRETS

And lay the rest at God's Feet.

Whichever Decision I Decide

To Submerge My Life In

Will be for Me and ONLY ME.

So, to my random OVERTHINKING:

Please Chill Out

AND LET A SISTAH BE.

Needless to say, it didn't. I received unconditional love from Kenny! Had me steeping in the name of love singing.

–K John-

"Now the tide is coming in

I see the waves flowing

Out there on the ocean

So don't leave me hanging.

I've been waiting too long.

For this moment, my ship has finally come."

It was at the dock waiting for me to board. I eagerly boarded, enjoying premium service. I was receiving all that I had ever asked for without asking. So why wasn't it enough to turn back on my switch and make it stick? Oh, I knew the answer. Guilt refused to leave me alone. However, this time in a different format. My heart is too genuine to give off energy. It's just that I had no natural desire to reciprocate in full capacity at that moment, the love I was being given. No way was I going to playhouse and fake it till I made it. Been there, done that! It seems as if I was just there to take. Enjoying all the perks that fell upon me. I wanted to soak it all in and continue to be the wind. Free as each breeze blowing in any which way it felt. If I was anything, I was real. It was time to cut ties and go the other way. Because I wanted love, I got it.

Hmmm, "Why was I so indecisive about giving it?" I asked myself.

After countless years of heartbreak, grief, and continuous healing, I am on this roller coaster full of beginnings and ends.

I'm bombarded with this thing Called Love.

I began to Isolate within myself.

Zigzagged in a Maze of Confusion.

Lost, unable to capture a Way Out.

Planted in the Traps of Delusion

I've set for myself.

Has my TRAUMATIC Memories

I lean on for further Expectations

Froze Me into a place

Where my choices Smile at Me?

(Cough)

I mean Discrepancies

One after the Other, Frowning at Me?

Has the Love I Lost, Fearful to Gain,

Shifted my indecisive mind into a

"YES!"

"It's My Time to SHINE."

Don't you know if you CAN'T get Jiggy with Me,

My Way.

You DON'T have to Stay.

Ready to be Alone

My Way or the Highway,

I SAY.

(Cough)

I mean, your WISH is My Command

As I Stretch Out My Hands

THEN BOOM!

Circumstances cause me to pull them Back Again.

You know this is ALL to Protect

You from Me.

(Cough)

I mean, Me from You.

What if this Triumph is NO FLUKE?

I've LOCKED the door on Love,

But my heart HOLDS the KEY that

You keep pulling out Bit by Bit

As you CONTINUE to Love Me.

It's EXHAUSTING, I know.

I Truly Love You WITH ALL MY MIGHT.

But I'm NOT 100% SURE You'll Do Right.

How do I even show you that I'm For You?

Hell, this COULD BE a show.

So what happens when the Curtains Hang

NO MORE?

I Love You, I DO,

Which is why I WON'T ALLOW,

Not Even Me to Hurt You.

Your Energy Screams.

This is getting to be TOO MUCH.

It seems I can't help it.

I'm Playing Tough.

But I understand Life... Is Life

As I Close My Eyes and SLOWLY Die Inside.

(Cough)

I mean, Celebrate Your Freedom.

I Opened My Eyes,

Wearing the SAME OLD Indecisive Disguise.

To My Me for Me,

PLEASE LET GO OF MY KEY.

Who was I kidding? Kenni did not listen to my ass! Love kept rolling in, and I was told that I was supposed to accept my blessing by absorbing it all in. Kenni never let go of my hand, no matter how many times I tried.

I'd joke upon my arrival, "Forgive me."

I wasn't in my right mind, "Oh, and you better believe, I tried again, and again, and again! Till finally, that all came to an end! I was filled up to the rim and back in action. The love poured out of me so easily! So fast, it scared me! Kenni was in awe of my reciprocation. Then I looked around to find myself in a serious conversation."

Dang it.

Did you do it again, Girl?

Show your Hand Full of stability,

Loyalty and Lots of if you DON'T get it,

I Got You?

Now ee! I Done Told You!

Have you been placed back on this Pedal Stool?

Balancing the Pieces of Your Heart,

You carefully Mended it Back Together in one hand?

Then the Void you filled for Kenni in the other?

Ugh! Yup!

I think you've done it again!

There you stand with a Mask of Excitement on your face

Wearing that Damn Superwoman Cape,

Ready to chase ALL Kenni's BLUES AWAY

Didn't you promise you were Done Saving?

That you were just Going to Enjoy

Someone coming to Save You?

Putting Your Mind at Ease

As ALL those Insecure Thoughts Seized.

What happened to Simply

Dancing the Night Away

For a Chance?

Letting Kenny pay a bill or two.

Don't you know you DON'T ask for much, Boo?

(Sigh)

You NEED a Whooping!

Because you have done it again!

Digging Bones out of the Grave

BEFORE they Disintegrate.

How DARE you take up Another Mission

When you deem yourself retired?

Retired from turning your FLAWS into Flowers?

Dressing the Thorns Up as Buds

WAITING to Blossom.

YOU'VE RETIRED!

Retired from Honey Coating your words

Just so they can Digest Easily.

REMEMBER WHO YOU ARE!

You are Unapologetically

YOU!

Every sad story ISN'T yours

To Turn Around.

Your hands DON'T ALWAYS BELONG

In the Giving Position.

But Receiving Sometimes

YOU ARE NOT

Nor will you EVER ALLOW yourself to be placed

ON THIS PEDAL STOOL AGAIN!

Do You Understand?

I shook My Head.

Oh, look at God! You've done it again.

Declared ALL to reciprocate your Energy

Or Let You Be!

However, I'm NOT you anymore.

You seem to be like this, Revolving Door.

So who knows?

Let's just Keep On Pushing.

And see how this thing called Life Goes.

I did! I got my stuff together and listened to the other side of my Gemini! She was ready to wear me out, honey. I couldn't risk a whooping, so I made myself clear to Kenni and all that was before, and those who might be after! After all, closed mouths don't get fed, right?

Contrary to Popular Belief.

I used to be a Fluid Giver.

You know,

Never basking in your presence empty-handed.

Happily carrying the load even when

I'm Short-Winded.

I wouldn't DARE leave you alone.

Couldn't Fathom doing you Wrong.

I guess you can say I had a bit of a
"Given Fixation."

Longing to Love
Your Open Wounds closed.

Desiring to Heal Your Broken Heart
With the Pieces of My Mind
That had been left in.

Constantly Pouring into You,
Creating an Overflow.

Chased away your Chaos,
Replaced It with Peace.

Give your DRAINED SOUL a jump start from
My Sparks of Energy.
Deliberately CONNECTING You to Me.

For Love and Light, I've Furnished
Presenting you with all the Solutions
Being Me, Making it do. What it do.

(Sigh)
Such a Hard Lesson I had to Learn.

Gone like Yesterday,

WITHOUT a Trace, you were.

My Breath Quickened.

My Soul on the Edge of the Ledge,

Overdosing on this "IDEA" of Love.

I Choked.

The mission I Devoured to fix you up

Enough to Love Me.

Unfastened by the Heimlich

With the Hands of God Himself.

Terrified my palette would be Tainted.

By the Chalky Truth.

I boldly took a Sip of Forgiveness

And SWALLOWED it whole.

For I am Royalty by Nature.

One of GOD'S Finest Creations.

Worthy of ALL the Silver and Gold

Molded into the Fruits of the Spirit,

One should feel EXTREMELY BLESSED to own.

I now require this Flower to be Watered Consistently

Into its overflow,

Drenching My Roots.

Won't you Help Transform

My soil into a Bigger Home

As I Grow with your Bare Hands

Full of Good Intentions.

I need you to SUBMIT TO GOD.

So you'll have assistance in Conquering Your Demons.

Bask in Peace, while you become it.

Dance!

To Your Favorite Song.

Be OK with Being Alone.

For I am ONLY an Enhancement

Of Your Entire Being

Reassuring You.

Yes, You Are Seen!

Let's Pour into each other

From the NEVER-ENDING

Fountain of God.

The One who has Washed

And Made Me New.

Leaving ABSOLUTELY NO RESIDUE.

Understand,

You MUST Love Me as I Love You.

OR DON'T BOTHER, BOO.

You know, With or Without You.

Ms... Rita will ALWAYS make it.

Do Exactly What It Needs To Do!

We went on with our lives. Reciprocation became our foundation while we continued to live life separately, but together! Giving love just because it felt good, because it was naturally fulfilling. My indecisiveness, engraved in me. I could say it's the Gemini in me. But it's in me, not on me, so it can't be taken! Kenni accepted all of me! I blew like the wind, inconsistent as can be! But there stood Kenni swaying in my gust like a kite. Sturdy and secure, I enjoyed the breeze as I blew in whichever direction I felt. This was indeed love, but for the first time, I was whole! So, the love I received was an addition. Which meant I didn't need it! Kenni had done so much work during the year we were dating. Growth glowed when those eyes smiled at me with an "I love you!" It's like all I could do was sing celebratory tunes as love flooded me, day in and day out!

"It's like yesterday

I didn't even know your name

Now today

You're always on my mind

I never could have predicted that I'd feel this way

You are a beautiful surprise

Intoxicated every time I hear your voice

You've got me on a natural high

It's almost like I didn't even have a choice

You are a beautiful surprise."

-India Arie-

This love isn't like any other love! It's free! We added to each other as much as we added to ourselves. I was freed from the bondage that I had locked myself in. Scared to truly love and be loved. But this was different. This love was a choice. One thing about it! I'd choose it repeatedly if it meant I could get my Me for Me!

EPILOGUE

Growing with Greif

"Darkness, bow down to the day, mountains

get up out our way!

Breaking out of yesterday!

We got a now thing coming!

We told that giant in our face. No, you're not greater than our faith.

Best believe us when we say...

We got a new thing coming!

-Elevation Worship!

TEN YEARS LATER

"Let's give it up for our next graduate! Ahkhim Ni'juel Felton-Davis!"

The crowd went wild. Cheers escaped the arena just as swiftly as they all slowly vanished, highlighting a familiar voice that soothed my soul.

"That's my Fat Baby. Yes, Daddy's baby did it."

"Lavarius!" I called out.

Looking around our balcony view full of family and friends, I spotted frozen figures trapped in time. There was nothing. Yet, claps echoed in celebration as I continuously heard his voice. My eyes dilated with pure bliss, zooming in on the stage. There, that Joker was. His chocolate still glistened. Smile still melted my heart. Belly still hung as his bowlegs quickly climbed the stairs. In one scoop, our baby boy flew into the air. His being planted on his shoulders awarded my mind with nostalgic memories. Their chuckles warmed my heart with the simultaneous slogans, "Yeah, Baby! Let's go!" The sweat dripping down his grey beard, combined with his heavy breathing, tickled me.

"Put that Lil Boy down, Otis!" I yelled.

"Ma'am?" Kenni questioned. I looked around in confusion.

"What in the world?" I whispered to myself.

"What's wrong, Ms. Dez?" Aiden asked. I had no words.

"Get your phones out," Jaylon warned, "His turn is coming up."

As I was brought back to reality, there pouted O'Brien, tugging at my leg.

"Grandma, up, please," he squealed out.

"Pappi, come and get your child." I laughed.

Naming him after Lavarius wasn't fitting. His hazelnut slinky tail took after me. Again, I heard the same words.

Let's give it up for our next graduate, Ahkhim Ni'juel Felton-Davis!" The crowd went wild.

"I'm so proud of him!" yelled Kenni.

"Let's go, Brother, let's go!" called out the boys.

Ms. Leeann and I should have been isolated in our own little section. Once we started the tears, they seemed to have poisoned the entire balcony. However, my tears were fueled by joy. I don't know where Lavarius came from or where he went to. But he was here. He showed up. For his Fat Baby. For himself. For this family.

Buying five acres for our family was the best thing we could have done. Everyone had their own separate space, yet we were together. We meet up for dinner after church on Sundays to eat and catch up. It was a blessing having so many folks over to celebrate a dream come true. Our baby boy had the hardest battle with grief in School. Trials and tribulations that came with High school triggered him in unspeakable ways. Losing the protagonist in his life became a common excuse. But God! He overcame it all and graduated with honors. Granted a full ride to Davidson College for his academics and basketball skills. Everyone was proud!

Over 175 guests stretched over the land, dancing, playing cards. Singing karaoke, playing bones, enjoying this celebration.

"Ahkhim, what do you want for dinner, Little Boy?" I asked jokingly.

"You already know, Mommy," he smiled, "Chicken and fries."

I smiled, glancing out the window to see Lavarius doing the Q-Dog Walk with Jaylon and his friends.

Laughing in gratitude, I spoke, "Oh Lawd. This is life," I kissed Kenni's cheek.

"In Jesus' Name!" Kenni replied.

"In Jesus' name!"

-THE END-

IN LOVING MEMORY OF LAVARIUS O'BRIAN DAVIS

"Big Country and Superman"

Alpha: April 27, 1992

Omega: March 4, 2023

"Everywhere I go, every smile I see, I know you are there, smiling back at me. Dancing in the moonlight, I know you are free because I can see your star shining down on me."

ABOUT THE AUTHOR

Dezarita Dashai is a three-time author, poet, and speaker. She is the proud owner and Teacher of Ms. Dezy House of Love Child Care. She is the Founder and Executive Director of a growing non-profit, LOVE, known as leaning on virtuous energy, geared towards the well-being of all youth in our community.

Dezarita is a wonderful mother of four handsome young men and one Doodle named Koda. When free from responsibilities. You can catch her dancing or simply basking in nature.

She believes that if you're going to be anything in life! Be free! Whatever that looks like to you!